PASTA

JANE STACEY

PHOTOGRAPHY BY

GENTL & HYERS

CollinsPublishersSanFrancisco

A Division of HarperCollins*Publishers*

First published in USA 1995 by Collins Publishers San Francisco
1160 Battery Street, San Francisco, CA 94111

PRODUCED BY SMALLWOOD & STEWART, INC., NEW YORK CITY

© 1995 Smallwood & Stewart, Inc.

EDITOR: David Ricketts
FOOD STYLING: Frances Boswell
PROP STYLING: Edward Kemper Design
BOOK DESIGN: Susi Oberhelman
DESIGN ASSISTANT: Pat Tan

Library of Congress Cataloging-in-Publication Data

Stacey, Jane.
    Pasta / Jane Stacey.
        p.   cm. — (The gourmet pantry)
    Includes index.
    ISBN 0-00-225021-7
    1. Cookery (Pasta)   I. Title.   II. Series.
TX809.M17S68   1995
641.8'22 — dc20   95-5953

PRINTED IN ITALY

10 9 8 7 6 5 4 3 2 1

CONTENTS

INTRODUCTION

The transformation of such simple ingredients as flour and water and eggs into something as sophisticated and satisfying as noodles seems almost magical. From this simple beginning comes a food so versatile and so universally enjoyed that it can truly be described as a "staple." Pasta appears in clear delicate broths, tossed with herb-spiked sauces, or coiled in perfect nests awaiting some other end. Noodles, pasta, or macaroni—whatever its name, people across generations and across many cultures have been making, enjoying, and sharing this delectable food for centuries.

The history of pasta is tangled with contradictions and confusion. Did pasta arrive in Italy from the Chinese via Marco Polo, or did it migrate from India and the Arab countries in the late Middle Ages via Mongol or Tartar slaves? Whatever the truth is, macaroni, as it was commonly called, was firmly established in the trading centers of Venice, Florence, and Genoa by the late Middle Ages. Early recipes even suggest that "poached paste" be accompanied with butter and grated cheese. And no doubt pasta recipes traveled with Catherine de Médicis and her staff of Italian chefs when she moved to France in 1533 to marry Henry II.

Today, cooking with pasta is more inviting than ever. An increasing variety of fresh foods and high-quality packaged ingredients, such as Mexican, Middle Eastern, and Asian spices, condiments, and seasonings, is now available to us. We can find Thai coconut milk, fresh bean sprouts, and several varieties of cultivated mushrooms along with different fresh herbs in many grocery stores. Greens no longer mean only plastic-wrapped heads of pale iceberg lettuce, but include chicories, endive and radicchio, mustard and beet greens, kale, Swiss chard, and baby greens. Even if imported cheeses are not readily available, high-quality domestic varieties can fill in the gaps. Dried beans are no longer "filler" foods, but have begun to be seen for the delicious, healthful foods they are, especially when paired with pasta. We are relying less on meat as a cornerstone for every meal.

When we free ourselves from the rules (pasta is a first course only, or tortellini is served in broth only), we can begin to have fun with the abundance we have been given.

This selection of pasta recipes is a starting point, a sampler of some of the possibilities. I hope it encourages you, as it has me, to expand your repertoire of pasta dishes, to experiment in a new place or two, and to share these gifts with family and friends.

GLOSSARY

ACINI

Acini de pepe, a tiny pasta shaped like peppercorns but much smaller, are used primarily in soups, but are also delicious in baked puddings.

AGNOLOTTI

A type of ravioli, these are a small half-moon–shaped stuffed pasta.

AL DENTE

Al dente, loosely translated, means "to the tooth," and most commonly refers to cooking pasta just to the point that it offers a slight resistance when bitten—firm but tender.

ALL-PURPOSE FLOUR

A blend of hard and soft wheats, this is the most commonly available flour. Hard wheat, used for both bread making and pasta doughs, contains a high proportion of gluten, the protein that makes dough elastic for kneading. Since soft wheat contains less gluten, it is best suited for making pastries and cakes with a tender crumb. Unbleached flour is recommended for pasta making.

ALPHABET PASTA (10)

The letters of the alphabet are eternally popular shapes in clear and hearty soups.

ANGEL HAIR

See *Capellini*.

BEAN THREADS (27)

Also called cellophane or glass noodles, these are very thin long strands made from mung beans, ranging from clear to white. Best used in oriental-style dishes, they can be either deep-fried until puffy and crisp or soaked in water until softened and used in broth-type soups.

BUCATINI

Similar to spaghetti, these are long, thin, hollow noodles. Because of their substantial size, they pair well with hearty meat sauces, like Bolognese, and rich creamy sauces.

BUCKWHEAT PASTA (22)

Gray-brown pasta, made from buckwheat flour, it is commonly used in Japanese cooking (called soba noodles). Though not interchangeable, whole-wheat pasta would be a good substitute.

CANNELLONI

To make cannelloni, precooked pasta squares are rolled into tubular shapes and stuffed with vegetable, seafood, meat, or cheese fillings, then baked. Traditionally they are blanketed with a coating of béchamel sauce to prevent them from drying out.

CAPELLINI (15)

The thinnest pasta, less than $1/16$ inch wide, capellini is best served with simple light sauces that won't tear the fine delicate strands.

CAVATELLI

Formed by pinching off small pieces of pasta dough by hand and rolling them into oblong seed-pearl shapes, these are usually served with butter and Parmesan cheese or light sauces.

CELLOPHANE NOODLES

See *Bean Threads*.

CONCHIGLIE (8, 11)

A shell-shaped pasta, these are made in a variety of sizes. Small shells are often used in soups, while the medium-size ones are good in baked pastas, such as Baked Macaroni (p. 73), or with cream-based seafood or vegetable sauces. Large shells are traditionally stuffed with a ricotta filling and served with a simple tomato sauce.

DRIED PASTA

Most store-bought pasta is made with just water and semolina, a flour coarsely ground from hard durum wheat (see *Semolina*). Many excellent imported and domestic brands are available.

DURUM FLOUR

Also called Semolina flour, durum flour is made from a hard wheat with a high proportion of gluten, making pasta dough elastic during kneading. While durum wheat flour makes the best pasta dough, it is not widely available through retail outlets; an Italian restaurant that makes its own pasta may sell you some.

EGG NOODLES (20, 23)

Dried egg noodles, as the name suggests, differ from dried Italian-style pasta in that they contain eggs. Ranging from broad and flat to thin and round, they are often used in soups, puddings, and casseroles. Fried egg noodles are popular in Chinese cooking.

ELBOW MACARONI (2)

Elbow-shaped dried pasta is the traditional choice for macaroni and cheese. Because of its size and shape, it can stand up to a variety of sauces and is often used in casseroles.

FARFALLE (4)

Farfalle is Italian for "butterflies" and refers to a small rectangular-shaped pasta, pinched in the center to make a butterfly or bow-tie shape. Use with a light cream-based sauce and for pasta primavera. The sauce should complement, rather than conceal, the bow-tie shape. Farfalle are also an excellent choice for clear broth soups and pasta salads.

FETTUCCINE (14)

Loosely translated, fettuccine means "little slices." A long, flat pasta cut into ¼- to ½-inch widths, this shape seems to go with almost any sauce: seafood, tomato, meat, vegetable, a simple olive oil with fresh herbs, and even strong-flavored chunky sauces.

FRESH PASTA

Increasingly more widely available, although still roughly double the price of dried, "fresh" pasta can now be found in many shapes and flavors in the refrigerator cases of supermarkets.

FUSILLI (7)

Both long spiral-shaped pasta and short corkscrew-shaped tubes (see *Rotelle*) are called fusilli. A good guideline for using long fusilli is not to hide the ringlets with large chunks of fish, meat, or vegetables, but to use smoother, simpler sauces. For the short fusilli, chunky sauces work well.

GLASS NOODLES (27)

See *Bean Threads*.

14

13

15

16

17

18

19

20

21

22

23

24

25

26

27

LINGUINE (17)

Linguine means "little tongues," and refers to a long, flat noodle about ⅛ inch wide. It's often served with seafood, though it seems to go well with practically any sauce, smooth or chunky.

LO MEIN NOODLES

These fresh Chinese noodles are made with flour and eggs or flour and water. Long flat noodles about the width of linguine, ⅛ inch or a bit wider, they are available at asian markets and sometimes in supermarket freezers. Lo mein noodles are served with oriental-style vegetable, meat, or seafood toppings as well as in clear broth soups.

MOSTACCIOLI

A short, straight, tubelike pasta, either ribbed or smooth, mostaccioli (the name means "moustaches") is often paired with chunky tomato-based meat or vegetable sauces, or served in baked pasta dishes.

MUNG BEAN NOODLES (27)

See *Bean Threads*.

ORECCHIETTE

Orecchiette means "little ears," and this small, half-circular-shaped pasta does resemble an ear. The shape lends itself to butter sauces, cream-style sauces, and other simple sauces such as tomato sauce and any of the pestos.

ORZO (5)

Orzo, a tiny rice-shaped pasta, is popular in Greek cooking. It works well in salads, puddings, and soups, adding texture.

PAPPARDELLE (13)

At 1-inch wide, pappardelle is the widest pasta noodle. Ragoûts, fricassees, and other robust dishes are often served over pappardelle.

PASTINA (3)

Any tiny pasta such as acini or stelline ("tiny stars") is considered pastina.

PENNE (6)

A short, tubelike pasta with diagonally cut ends, penne goes well with just about any sauce, particularly tomato-based ones. Its firm texture is ideal for salads.

RADIATORE (9)

This short curly-edged pasta is sometimes described as resembling an old-fashioned heating radiator. Its ridges makes it perfect for pestos, tomato sauces, and cream sauces.

RAVIOLI (26)

Ravioli are stuffed pasta, most often small, square, or round and sometimes half-moon–shaped. They can be stuffed with cheese, meat, fish, or vegetable fillings and are served with many varieties of sauces. Dessert ravioli are filled with sweet fillings.

RAVIOLI FORMS

Ravioli forms are metal or plastic trays with hollowed indentations to form the ravioli shape. A sheet of pasta dough is placed on the form and the filling is added in dollops, centered in the indentations formed by the hollows. A second sheet is placed over the filled first sheet, and a rolling pin is used to press and seal the sheets together, cutting the ravioli into squares.

RICE NOODLES

All manner of shapes and sizes of rice noodles, made from rice flour and water, are available in oriental markets. They are generally long and cylindrical (shaped like spaghetti) and vary in thickness. Their length symbolizes longevity. Rice noodles are most commonly used in soups with clear broth.

RIGATONI (1)

A short, hollow, tubelike pasta, often with a ridged rather than smooth exterior, this firm-textured pasta holds up well to meat sauces and heavier tomato sauces. Mezzani (18) is similar to rigatoni but without the ridges.

ROTELLE

Generally, these are short twists or tight corkscrews, although pasta in the shape of wagon wheels is also sometimes called rotelle. Both shapes are great for capturing vinai-grettes, cream sauces, and simple sauces such as pestos. It is often available in packages of mixed colors, such as spinach green, tomato red, and beet red, which makes it especially attractive in salads and soups.

SEMOLINA

A flour made from durum wheat, semolina is yellowish in color and a bit coarser ground than regular flour, though not as coarse as corn-meal. Its high gluten content makes it excellent for pasta making. Do not use semolina in an electric extrusion pasta machine (unless specified by the manufacturer), as it will clog the machine.

SPAGHETTI/SPAGHETTINI (24, 25)

The most familiar pasta, spaghetti is a long, thin cylindrical pasta that marries well with oil-based sauces, cream and butter sauces, and seafood sauces. In Italy, it is rarely served with a meat sauce. Spaghettini, a very thin form of spaghetti, does better with lighter sauces and toppings.

SPECIALTY PASTAS

Corn, Jerusalem artichoke, quinoa, buckwheat, potato, and sweet potato pastas are available for those who choose not to eat wheat-based pastas. Their textures and tastes vary.

TAGLIATELLE (21)

Cut ¾ inch in width, these long flat noodles are wider than fettuccine, and slightly narrower than pappardelle. Classically served with meat sauces, tagliatelle, like fettuccine, seems to go with almost any sauce.

TORTELLINI (12)

Tortellini are a small stuffed pasta, made by spooning a little stuffing onto small circles of dough, folding them first in half, and then pulling the ends of the half-circles together and pressing them to seal. They are served in soups and pasta salads and with vegetable sauces, pestos, tomato sauces, cream-based sauces, and melted butter with Parmesan cheese.

UDON NOODLES (19)

Udon are thick white noodles made from flour, water, and salt. To make the stiff dough pliable, traditionally the Japanese noodle-maker stomps on the dough with bare feet (the dough is covered, of course). There are many types of udon noodles, but they are generally served in hearty broths.

VERMICELLI (16)

Vermicelli are very thin spaghetti-like noodles, often sold shaped into little nests. Because of their fragile texture, vermicelli are best served in broth-type soups or with simple sauces such as melted butter or olive oil and herbs. Be careful, since even the slightest tossing causes the noodles to break.

ZITI

Available in various lengths and sizes, ziti are medium-size hollow tubes of dried pasta. They are ideal for creamy sauces and tomato sauces. Large ziti are sometimes stuffed.

MAKING PASTA WITH AN ELECTRIC EXTRUSION TYPE MACHINE

EGG PASTA

SERVES 6

Enough for eighty 2-inch ravioli; two dozen cannelloni; or two 13-by 9-inch pans of lasagne.

3¼ cups all-purpose flour
½ teaspoon salt
5 medium-size eggs, lightly beaten

To prepare the dough: Place the flour and salt in the bowl of the pasta machine. Turn the machine on for 30 seconds to 1 minute to blend well. Pour the eggs into a 2-cup liquid measuring cup with a spout. With the pasta machine turned on, slowly add the eggs, pouring in about 1 tablespoon at a time, letting the flour gradually absorb the eggs. (Take 1 full minute to add the eggs.) Then let the dough knead for 5 minutes.

Stop the machine and lift the lid to check the dough's consistency: It should be very firm and broken into pieces about 1½ inches in diameter. A dough that is too wet will look almost smooth with no floury appearance at all and may have formed a ball or several large chunks in the bowl. In this case, turn on the machine, add more flour 1 tablespoon at a time, and let it knead until the flour is well incorporated.

If the dough is too dry, there will be some crumbly, floury bits at the bottom of the bowl; add water 1 teaspoon at a time, with the machine running, letting the dough absorb the water. Once the proper consistency is reached, let the machine knead the dough for 4 to 6 minutes before extruding the pasta.

To extrude the dough: Fit the appropriate die or disk into the machine. Place a baking sheet lightly dusted with flour under the extruder. With a sharp paring knife, cut the pasta as it extrudes to the desired lengths and lay on the baking sheet. The first 10 to 15 inches of extruded pasta will have a dry, flaky appearance; it should be returned to the bowl and extruded again. If the pasta continues to look ragged and flaky, it may not be thoroughly kneaded or may be too dry. Let the dough rest in the bowl of the pasta machine with the cover on for 15 minutes or so, then knead the dough for 3 to 4 minutes. If it is still too flaky, add additional water and try again.

If the pasta sticks together as it extrudes, it is too wet. Add flour, 1 tablespoon at a time, stopping the machine and checking the dough's consistency. Then let the dough knead for several minutes before extruding it.

Cut the dough into 12- to 14-inch lengths for long pastas and 1- to 2-inch lengths for macaroni.

The pasta can be cooked immediately (for best texture) or left to dry for later use. To store the pasta cover the baking sheet with plastic wrap and refrigerate until ready to cook. Use the pasta within a day or two for the best results.

The recipes for the flavored pasta variations that follow will make only about half as much pasta as the plain pasta recipe, or about 3 servings. As a result, you will need to make two batches of the flavored pasta to use for those recipes in the book that make 6 to 8 servings.

RED PEPPER PASTA

3 cups all-purpose flour

½ teaspoon salt

½ cup puréed, peeled, seeded, roasted
    red bell pepper (p. 20)

1 large egg plus 1 large egg yolk

Prepare the pasta dough (p. 12), adding the pepper purée to the flour and salt and letting it mix for a minute or two before adding the eggs.

SPINACH PASTA

2½ cups all-purpose flour

½ cup cooked spinach, chopped very fine
    & squeezed dry

¼ teaspoon salt

2 large eggs

Prepare the pasta dough (p. 12), then add the spinach to the flour and salt. Let it mix for a minute before adding the eggs.

TOMATO PASTA

2 cups plus 2 tablespoons all-purpose flour

¼ cup plus 1 tablespoon tomato paste

2 large eggs

¼ teaspoon salt

Prepare the pasta dough (p. 12), adding the tomato paste to the flour and salt. Let it mix a minute or two before adding the eggs.

TO COOK PASTA

In a large pot, bring a generous amount of water, as much as a quart per serving of pasta, to a rolling boil over high heat. Drop the pasta into the boiling water (salt and oil are unnecessary) and stir once or twice to ensure that the noodles are separated and well dispersed in the pot, and bring back to a boil.

Fresh capellini cooks almost instantly. Test wider and thicker noodles for doneness after 2 or 3 minutes. Dried pasta may take as much as 12 minutes to cook. The best test is to remove a strand or two from the boiling water, let cool slightly, and bite into the pasta. There should be no dry, hard center; the noodles should be firm to the bite, not mushy. Drain the pasta immediately in a colander. Serve the pasta according to your recipe.

MAKING PASTA BY HAND

EGG PASTA

SERVES 3 TO 4

This recipe makes enough dough for three dozen 2-inch ravioli, one dozen cannelloni, one 13- by 9-inch pan of lasagne, or one 16- by 16- inch sheet of pasta. You will need to make two batches to use in those recipes that make 6 to 8 servings.

2 cups all-purpose flour

½ teaspoon salt

2 large eggs

2 teaspoons olive oil

To prepare the dough: Mound the flour on a lightly floured work surface. Mix in the salt. Using a pastry scraper, mound the mixture and make a well in the center. Lightly beat the eggs and olive oil in a small bowl. Pour the egg mixture into the well, and with a fork or your fingers, gradually incorporate the flour into the eggs.

To knead the dough: When the flour and eggs start to form a ball, firmly press any dry, flaky dough pieces into the mass. The dough will seem very rough and dry in texture, and feel very solid. Continue to knead in any clumps of dough, then set the dough to the side and scrape the work surface clean. Lightly flour it again, and wash and dry your hands.

The dough will be very, very stiff, so kneading will take some work. Push against the dough with the heel of your hand, fold it back over itself or push it into a ball, and turn it. Continue kneading until the dough becomes smooth but still dense, almost claylike.

Knead for a full 10 minutes; you can let the dough rest, covered, on the work surface when you get tired. Resting the dough allows the gluten (strands of protein in the wheat) to relax a bit and makes kneading easier. When the dough is almost completely smooth, wrap it in plastic wrap and let stand for at least 1 hour and up to 2 or 3 hours.

To shape the dough: Place the pasta dough on a lightly floured surface. A long, straight wooden rolling pin is best for rolling. Roll the dough out to about ¹⁄₁₆ inch thick, sliding and turning the dough and keeping the work surface very lightly floured as you roll to prevent sticking.

To achieve the necessary thinness, roll and stretch the dough simultaneously. Push down against the rolling pin as you press the pin against the dough and away from you, stretching it slightly as well as rolling it as you push. Use your whole weight to push. Continue to push, roll, and stretch the dough until it is nearly paper-thin. When the dough is as thin as possible, let it rest for several minutes. It should no longer be sticky, but it should still be pliable.

Dust the dough lightly with flour before cutting it. Cut the dough into lasagne noodles or sheets for ravioli. To cut the dough into ribbons, use a pastry cutter to cut the dough into even widths, or fold the dough loosely into a roll 3 to 4 inches across, and use a sharp knife to cut the roll into strips of even widths. Be sure to press down with the knife quickly and evenly to produce even noodles. After the roll is cut, unroll the noodles so they can dry evenly.

SOME PASTA WIDTHS

PAPPARDELLE — 1 inch

TAGLIATELLE — ¾ inch

FETTUCCINE — ¼ to ½ inch

LINGUINE — about ⅛ inch

CAPELLINI OR ANGEL HAIR — less than ¹⁄₁₆ inch

FRESH HERB PASTA

Prepare pasta dough (p. 14), adding ¾ cup coarsely chopped mixed fresh herbs, such as chives, parsley, thyme, or basil to the flour and salt mixture before adding the eggs.

CRACKED BLACK PEPPER PASTA

Prepare pasta dough (p. 14) adding 2 teaspoons fresh coarsely ground black pepper to the flour and salt mixture before adding the eggs.

BASIL PESTO

THERE ARE MANY VARIETIES OF BASIL, EACH WITH
ITS OWN NUANCES OF COLOR AND FLAVOR, RANGING FROM MINTY
TO DISTINCTIVELY LICORICE FLAVORED. THE
ADDITION OF PARSLEY LEAVES KEEPS THE COLOR BRIGHT, WHILE
THE LEMON JUICE ENHANCES ALL THE FLAVORS.

Combine the basil, parsley, Parmesan, lemon juice, and garlic in a food processor fitted with the metal blade and process until blended. With the machine running, add the olive oil in a steady stream, stopping the machine every so often to scrape down the side of the bowl with a rubber spatula, and process just until the mixture is a coarse purée; overblending will make the sauce thin and watery. To store, cover tightly and refrigerate for up to two days.

1 cup packed fresh basil

¼ cup packed fresh
   flat-leaf parsley

3 tablespoons freshly grated
   Parmesan cheese

1 tablespoon fresh lemon juice

3 garlic cloves, minced

⅓ cup olive oil

SERVING SUGGESTIONS

- Add 1 to 2 tablespoons pesto for each 3- to 4-ounce serving of hot cooked pasta and toss. Any sturdy long pasta works well; thin pastas such as capellini tend to break easily. Or use pesto with most short tube shapes, such as ziti or penne, as well as conchiglie, rotelle, and radiatore. Pesto is not well suited to tiny pastas such as orzo or pastina.

- Stir a few tablespoons into soups, creamy salad dressings or vinaigrettes, mayonnaise, pasta salads, potato salads, or omelets.

- Spoon on crostini with chunked tomatoes, bell pepper strips, and fresh mozzarella.

SPINACH PESTO

THIS VERSION OF PESTO MIXES SPINACH WITH BASIL,
RESULTING IN A MILDER FLAVOR THAN REGULAR BASIL PESTO.
TOASTED WALNUTS ARE AN ECONOMICAL REPLACEMENT
FOR THE MORE TRADITIONAL PINE NUT, AND GIVE THE PESTO
A SLIGHTLY CHUNKY TEXTURE.

½ cup walnut pieces

3 cups packed fresh spinach leaves,
    rinsed & drained

½ cup fresh packed basil

3 tablespoons freshly grated
    Parmesan cheese

1 tablespoon fresh lemon juice

3 garlic cloves, minced

¾ cup olive oil

In a small skillet, toast the walnuts over medium heat, stirring often, for 2 to 3 minutes, or until they begin to brown and become aromatic. Transfer the nuts to a plate to cool.

In a large saucepan, combine the spinach and ¼ cup water and cook, covered, over high heat, for 30 to 45 seconds, or just until the leaves are wilted. Drain well. When the spinach is cool enough to handle, squeeze dry.

Prepare the pesto using the same method as for Basil Pesto (p. 17).

SERVING SUGGESTIONS

- Add 2 to 3 tablespoons of this chunky pesto for each 3- to 4-ounce serving of hot cooked pasta and toss. Use flat long pastas such as linguine, fettuccine, or tagliatelle.
- For a creamier pesto-based sauce, combine 1 cup pesto, ½ cup chicken broth, and ¾ cup ricotta cheese in a saucepan and stir over medium heat until bubbly. Toss the sauce with 12 to 16 ounces of hot cooked pasta, for 4 servings, and serve immediately, garnished with additional fresh basil leaves and/or toasted walnuts.

SUN-DRIED TOMATO PESTO

MAKES 1 1/2 CUPS, OR 10 TO 12 SERVINGS

A WHOLE NEW TASTE, AND A NICE ALTERNATIVE
IN THOSE MONTHS WHEN FRESH BASIL IS UNAVAILABLE,
THIS INTENSELY FLAVORED PESTO
PAIRS WELL WITH SHORTER-SHAPED PASTA SUCH
AS PENNE, FUSILLI, AND ROTELLE.

Preheat the oven to 350°F. Spread the bread crumbs on a baking sheet and toast in the oven, stirring occasionally, for 8 to 10 minutes, or until they are lightly browned.

In a small nonreactive saucepan, combine the sun-dried tomatoes and wine and bring to a boil over medium heat. Remove the saucepan from the heat and let stand for 5 to 10 minutes, or until the tomatoes are plump and softened. Drain, reserving the liquid for a salad dressing or sauce.

In a food processor fitted with the metal blade, combine the toasted bread crumbs, sun-dried tomatoes, garlic, Parmesan, and the oregano and rosemary if desired. Proceed as for Basil Pesto (p. 17). Tightly covered and stored in the refrigerator, the pesto will keep up to one week.

½ cup fresh bread crumbs

1 cup sun-dried tomatoes (not oil-packed)

½ cup dry white wine

2 garlic cloves, minced

2 tablespoons freshly grated Parmesan cheese

½ teaspoon minced fresh oregano (optional)

½ teaspoon minced fresh rosemary (optional)

½ cup olive oil

SERVING SUGGESTIONS

• Add a tablespoon or 2 of pesto to each 3- to 4-ounce serving of hot cooked pasta and toss.

• A tablespoon of pesto will enliven a bland tomato sauce or perk up a plain vinaigrette.

• Spread pesto very thinly on chicken breasts before grilling or broiling, or serve as a condiment with sliced cooked turkey breast.

ROASTED RED BELL PEPPER SAUCE

MAKES 1 1/2 CUPS, OR 4 TO 6 SERVINGS

THE PUNGENT FLAVOR OF ROASTED BELL PEPPERS MAKES
THIS A DELICIOUS ALTERNATIVE TO MORE COMMON TOMATO-BASED
PASTA SAUCES. STIR A FEW TABLESPOONS INTO YOUR
FAVORITE TOMATO SAUCE TO DEEPEN ITS FLAVOR. FOR A GOLDEN-COLORED
VARIATION, USE YELLOW BELL PEPPERS.

3 red bell peppers

2 tablespoons olive oil

1 garlic clove, minced

½ cup chicken broth

3 tablespoons unsalted butter, at
    room temperature (optional)

Prepare the roasted peppers: Preheat the broiler, and place the peppers on a pan 6 inches from the heat source. Roast the peppers, turning frequently, for about 15 minutes, or until their skins is charred and wrinkled. The peppers can also be roasted on a grill, or over a gas flame. Place the peppers in a paper bag, put the paper bag in a plastic bag, and seal. When cool enough to handle, halve the peppers lengthwise and core, seed, and peel them. Cut them into ½-inch-wide strips and set aside a few strips for garnish.

In a medium-size skillet, heat the olive oil over medium heat. Add the minced garlic and cook, stirring, without letting it brown, for 30 to 45 seconds, or until it is softened and very aromatic. Add the bell pepper strips and broth and cook, covered, for 2 to 3 minutes.

Scrape the mixture into a food processor fitted with the metal blade and process until smooth; or leave slightly chunky if you prefer. For a smoother sauce, pour the mixture into a sieve placed over a bowl, and force it through with the back of a spoon. For a rich finish, stir in the butter. To serve, garnish with the reserved red pepper strips. To store, cover tightly and refrigerate for two or three days.

UNCOOKED FRESH TOMATO SAUCE

MAKES 3 CUPS, OR 4 TO 6 SERVINGS

AS WITH ALL FRESH TOMATO SAUCES, PLUM OR ROMA

TOMATOES ARE PREFERRED SINCE THEY ARE "MEATIER." SAVE THIS

RECIPE FOR THE SUMMER MONTHS WHEN BASIL AND

TOMATOES ARE AT THEIR BEST. THIS SAUCE IS SO VERSATILE IT CAN

BE USED ON MOST ANY PASTA SHAPE.

1 ½ pounds ripe tomatoes,
    preferably plum or Roma

2 tablespoons olive oil

1 tablespoon extra-virgin olive oil

2 garlic cloves, minced

1 tablespoon balsamic vinegar

6 to 8 fresh basil leaves,
    coarsely chopped

Salt & freshly ground
    black pepper to taste

To peel the tomatoes, bring a large pot of water to a boil. Slip the tomatoes into the boiling water and blanch for about 30 seconds. With a slotted spoon, remove the tomatoes and place in a bowl of cold water. Drain and peel off the loosened skins. To seed the tomatoes, cut them in half crosswise, and squeeze gently to remove the seeds.

In a medium-size bowl, combine all the ingredients. Let stand at room temperature for 1 hour to allow the flavors to mingle. Use this sauce the day it is made.

VARIATIONS

- Add 10 to 12 pitted Calamata or other brine-cured olives.
- Add 1 tablespoon rinsed and drained capers.
- Add 3 mashed anchovy fillets.
- Add any combination or all of the above.

FRESH TOMATO SAUCE

MAKES 3 CUPS, OR 8 SERVINGS

THIS BARELY COOKED, SUN-RIPENED TOMATO SAUCE IS
BOTH EASY AND VERSATILE: TOSS IT WITH FRESH PASTA, SPREAD IT
ON CROSTINI, OR USE IT AS A TOPPING FOR GRILLED FISH.
THE BALSAMIC VINEGAR ADDS A HINT OF DARK SWEETNESS TO
BALANCE THE TOMATO'S NATURAL ACIDITY.

In a medium-size nonreactive skillet, heat the oil over medium heat. Add the onion and garlic and cook, stirring, for about 1 minute, or until the onion begins to soften. Add the tomatoes, wine, and vinegar and cook, stirring frequently, for 3 to 4 minutes, or until slightly thickened. Remove the skillet from the heat. Stir in the basil and season with the salt and pepper. To store, cover tightly and refrigerate for up to two days.

3 tablespoons olive oil

½ onion, chopped medium-fine

2 garlic cloves, minced

1½ pounds ripe tomatoes,
  preferably plum, peeled,
  seeded & coarsely chopped
  (p. 22)

¼ cup dry white wine

2 teaspoons balsamic vinegar

6 to 8 fresh basil leaves,
  coarsely chopped

Salt & freshly ground black
  pepper to taste

ROASTED TOMATO SAUCE

THIS INTENSELY FLAVORED SAUCE IS
SPIKED WITH HOT PEPPER FLAKES. IT IS DELICIOUS
OVER FISH AS WELL AS ON PASTA. IF YOU
USE YELLOW TOMATOES YOU WILL HAVE A SLIGHTLY
SWEETER GOLDEN-HUED SAUCE.

2 pounds ripe tomatoes,
    preferably plum, halved

½ red bell pepper, cored
    & seeded

½ onion, coarsely chopped

¼ cup olive oil

¼ teaspoon hot pepper flakes

½ cup dry red wine

Salt & freshly ground black
    pepper to taste

Preheat the oven to 425°F. In a medium-size bowl, combine the tomatoes, bell pepper, onion, oil, and hot pepper flakes and toss until the vegetables are well coated with oil. Transfer the mixture to a 13- by 9-inch baking pan. Bake, uncovered, for 25 minutes, or until the vegetables are beginning to brown.

Sprinkle the wine over the roasted vegetables and season with salt and pepper.

Scrape the vegetable mixture into a food processor fitted with the metal blade and process until smooth. Strain through a medium sieve, pushing the sauce through with the back of a spoon, and discard the solids. The sauce keeps, covered and refrigerated, for up to four days.

MINESTRONE

IF YOU DON'T HAVE HOMEMADE BROTH ON HAND,
USE LOW-SALT CANNED CHICKEN BROTH OR A HEARTY VEGETABLE
STOCK. THE CHOICE OF VEGETABLES AND BEANS
IS ALMOST LIMITLESS—CHOOSE THOSE THAT LOOK MOST
APPEALING AT THE MARKET.

In a large nonreactive pot, heat the olive oil over medium-high heat. Add the onion and garlic and cook, stirring often, for 2 to 3 minutes, or until the onion is softened. Stir in the celery, carrots, and turnip or rutabaga, and cook, stirring occasionally, for about 5 minutes, or until slightly softened. Stir in the cabbage, Swiss chard, and green beans. Add 8 cups broth and the ham bone or hock if desired and bring to a boil. Reduce the heat to medium-low and simmer for 10 to 15 minutes.

Add the tomatoes, kidney beans, chick-peas, and herbs and simmer for about 40 minutes, or until all the vegetables are cooked through. Add more broth as necessary to keep the vegetables covered.

Meanwhile, cook the pasta following the basic method (p. 13), or according to the package directions, until al dente, firm but tender. Drain well.

Remove the ham bone from the soup if using, and discard. Season the soup with salt and pepper.

Divide the pasta among heated soup bowls and ladle the hot soup over the pasta. Serve immediately and pass the Parmesan.

¼ cup olive oil

1 onion, chopped

4 garlic cloves, minced

2 celery stalks, chopped

2 carrots, cut in ⅛-inch-thick slices

1 small turnip or rutabaga, peeled & cut into ½-inch dice

4 cups loosely packed thinly sliced green cabbage

4 cups loosely packed thinly sliced Swiss chard

2 cups chopped green beans

8 to 10 cups chicken broth

1 small ham bone or smoked ham hock (optional)

1 (14½-ounce) can whole tomatoes in juice, drained & coarsely chopped

1 (15-ounce) can kidney beans, drained & rinsed

1 (15-ounce) can chick-peas, drained & rinsed

½ cup minced fresh parsley

1 tablespoon minced fresh sage

2 teaspoons minced fresh thyme

2 teaspoons minced fresh oregano

1 to 1½ cups dried pasta shapes, such as wheels or bow-ties

Freshly grated Parmesan cheese

LEMONY LETTUCE, ORZO & GREEN PEA SOUP

SERVES 6

ORZO, A TINY RICE-SHAPED PASTA, WORKS
ESPECIALLY WELL HERE SINCE IT REMAINS FIRMER
THAN RICE AND HOLDS ITS SHAPE BETTER.
SERVE THE SOUP THE DAY IT IS MADE TO RETAIN ITS
BRIGHT TASTE AND COLOR.

¾ cup orzo

3 tablespoons butter

½ cup minced shallots

5 cups chicken broth

½ cup dry white wine

3 cups frozen green peas

4 cups shredded lettuce,
    such as green leaf,
    romaine, or iceberg

1 teaspoon minced fresh thyme

1 teaspoon grated lemon zest

2 tablespoons fresh lemon juice

Salt & freshly ground black
    pepper to taste

Fresh thyme leaves,
    for garnish

Cook the orzo following the basic method (p. 13) until al dente. Drain well, and set aside.

In a 4-quart nonreactive stockpot or saucepan, melt the butter over medium heat. Add the shallots and cook, stirring, for 2 to 3 minutes, or until softened. Add the broth, wine, peas, lettuce, and minced thyme. Bring to a boil, reduce the heat, and simmer, uncovered, for 15 minutes.

Strain the soup through a sieve into a large heatproof bowl. Working in batches, spoon the cooked vegetables into a food processor fitted with the metal blade and process, adding just enough broth to make a smooth purée.

Return the puréed vegetables and broth to the pot and gently reheat the soup. Stir in the lemon zest and juice and season with the salt and pepper.

To serve, spoon ¼ cup cooked orzo into heated serving bowls. Ladle in the soup and garnish with fresh thyme leaves.

PASTA WITH OLIVE OIL, GARLIC & HOT PEPPER FLAKES

EXTRA-VIRGIN OLIVE OIL ISN'T OFTEN USED FOR COOKING
BECAUSE IT TENDS TO OVERWHELM OTHER FLAVORS. HERE IT IS MIXED
WITH PURE OLIVE OIL FOR A MILDER RESULT. TOSS THIS
SIMPLEST OF ALL PASTA SAUCES WITH ANY LONG PASTA: SPAGHETTI,
SPAGHETTINI, AND CAPELLINI ARE TRADITIONAL.

¼ cup olive oil

¼ cup extra-virgin olive oil

8 garlic cloves, minced

2 teaspoons hot pepper flakes

4 teaspoons minced fresh
flat-leaf parsley

1 teaspoon minced fresh
oregano

1 teaspoon minced fresh
rosemary

1 teaspoon minced fresh
thyme

12 ounces fresh or dried long
pasta such as spaghetti,
spaghettini, or capellini

Salt & freshly ground black
pepper to taste

In a small skillet, heat the olive oils over medium heat. Stir in the garlic, hot pepper flakes, and the fresh herbs. Remove from the heat.

Meanwhile, cook the pasta following the basic method (p. 13) until al dente. Drain well.

Toss the oil and herb mixture with the hot cooked pasta, season with salt and pepper. Serve immediately in heated bowls.

PASTA WITH
LEMON-MASCARPONE SAUCE

SERVES 4

MASCARPONE IS A CREAMY, FRESH COW'S MILK CHEESE
WITH A SLIGHTLY SWEET FLAVOR. WELL KNOWN AS AN INGREDIENT
IN TIRAMISÙ, MASCARPONE MELTS BEAUTIFULLY TO
MAKE A SIMPLE SAUCE FOR PASTA. USE A LONG, FLAT PASTA SUCH
AS TAGLIATELLE OR FETTUCCINE.

In a medium-size nonreactive skillet, whisk together the wine, Parmesan, thyme, lemon zest, and mascarpone over medium-high heat until smooth and hot. Season with the salt and pepper.

Meanwhile, cook the pasta following the basic method (p. 13) until al dente. Drain well. Toss the sauce with the hot cooked pasta. Serve immediately in heated bowls.

¼ cup dry white wine

¼ cup freshly grated
   Parmesan cheese

1 teaspoon minced fresh thyme

2 teaspoons grated lemon zest

1 cup mascarpone

Salt & freshly ground black
   pepper to taste

12 ounces fresh or
   dried long pasta

VARIATIONS
- Omit the lemon zest and add 1 teaspoon minced garlic.
- Omit the white wine and lemon zest and add 3 tablespoons dry marsala.
- Omit the thyme and lemon zest and add 1 tablespoon minced fresh basil.

PASTA WITH CANNELLINI
BEANS & SAGE

CANNELLINI ARE WHITE KIDNEY-SHAPED BEANS
WITH A SOFT, CREAMY TEXTURE. WHEN TOSSED WITH HOT PASTA,
THE BUTTERY TASTING BEANS, RICH OLIVE OIL,
AND THE PEPPERY SAGE FLAVOR BLEND TOGETHER TO MAKE THIS
SIMPLE DISH MORE THAN THE SUM OF ITS PARTS.

In a large skillet, heat the oils over medium-high heat. Add the garlic and cook, stirring often, for 30 to 45 seconds, or until very aromatic. Stir in the beans, minced sage, and ½ cup water, and bring to a boil. Reduce the heat to low and simmer for 10 to 15 minutes. If the mixture seems too dry, add a little more water or some pasta cooking water. Season with the salt and pepper.

Meanwhile, cook the pasta following the basic method (p. 13) until al dente. Drain well.

Add the hot pasta to the bean mixture and toss gently to combine. Divide the pasta among heated bowls and garnish with sage leaves.

3 tablespoons extra-virgin olive oil

2 tablespoons olive oil

3 garlic cloves, thinly sliced

2½ cups cooked cannellini beans or 2 (15-ounce) cans cannellini beans, drained & rinsed

1 tablespoon minced fresh sage

Salt & freshly ground black pepper to taste

12 ounces dried rigatoni, penne, or ziti

4 whole sage leaves, for garnish

INDIAN CAULIFLOWER & CHICK-PEAS WITH PENNE

SERVES 4

GARAM MASALA IS AN INDIAN SPICE BLEND AVAILABLE
IN SOME GOURMET FOOD SHOPS, ALTHOUGH IT'S EASY ENOUGH TO
MAKE FRESH AT HOME. COOKING IN TEA RATHER THAN
BROTH OR WATER IS AN OLD INDIAN STREET VENDOR'S TRICK
AND THE RESULT IS SUBTLE AND DELICIOUS.

GARAM MASALA

1 teaspoon coriander seeds

½ teaspoon cumin seeds

½ teaspoon ground cinnamon

¼ teaspoon whole cloves

¼ teaspoon grated nutmeg

½ bay leaf

½ teaspoon cumin seeds

3 to 4 cups cauliflower florets

¼ cup vegetable oil

1 onion, slivered

3 garlic cloves, minced

2 cups diced (½-inch) peeled
   eggplant

1 jalapeño or serrano pepper,
   cored, seeded & diced
   (optional)

1 cup cooked chick-peas or
   1 cup canned chick-peas,
   drained & rinsed

1 cup brewed black tea or water

Salt & freshly ground black
   pepper to taste

12 ounces dried penne

3 tablespoons chopped fresh
   cilantro

Prepare the garam masala: In a spice grinder, or using a mortar and pestle, grind all the ingredients into a fine powder. Set aside ¾ teaspoon for this recipe and store the remainder, tightly covered, in a cool, dark place.

In a skillet, toast the cumin seeds over medium heat, stirring occasionally, for about 1 minute, or until lightly browned. Transfer to a plate to cool.

In a medium-size saucepan of boiling water, blanch the cauliflower for about 2 minutes, or until just cooked but not soft. Drain and rinse under cold running water to stop the cooking. Set aside.

In a large nonreactive skillet, heat the oil over medium heat. Add the onion and garlic and cook, stirring, for 1 to 2 minutes, or until the onion begins to soften. Add the eggplant, cumin seeds, and chile pepper if desired, and cook, stirring often, for about 3 minutes. Stir in the cauliflower and chick-peas, then stir in the tea or water and the reserved garam masala, and cook for 5 to 7 minutes, or until the eggplant has softened and the sauce has thickened slightly. Season with the salt and pepper. Keep warm.

Meanwhile, cook the pasta following the basic method (p. 13) until al dente. Drain. Return the pasta to the pot, add the cauliflower mixture and cilantro, and toss gently to coat. Divide among heated pasta bowls and serve immediately.

LINGUINE WITH FENNEL, OLIVES & SHAVED ASIAGO

SERVES 4 TO 6

SWEET RED ONIONS, SALTY OLIVES, AND CRUNCHY FENNEL COMBINE
BEAUTIFULLY WITH BLACK PEPPER LINGUINE AND SHARP ASIAGO CHEESE IN
THIS DISH AND SPLASHES OF SHERRY VINEGAR AND SWEET APPLE CIDER
QUICKLY REDUCE TO MAKE ITS SIMPLE SAUCE. IF ASIAGO IS NOT AVAILABLE,
USE SHAVED OR SHREDDED PARMESAN, ROMANO, OR FETA.

In a large nonreactive skillet, heat the oil over medium-high heat. Add the fennel and red onion and cook, stirring often, for 5 to 7 minutes, or until the onion is softened and the fennel is crisp-tender. Add the apple cider and sherry vinegar, reduce the heat to medium, and stir in the olives and oregano. Cook for 1 to 2 minutes, or until the juices have thickened slightly. Season with the salt and pepper and keep warm.

Meanwhile, cook the pasta following the basic method (p. 13) until al dente. Drain well.

Add the pasta to the sauce and toss to combine. Divide the pasta and vegetables among heated serving bowls and top with the shaved Asiago and parsley. Garnish with oregano sprigs, if desired. Serve immediately.

3 tablespoons olive oil

1 large fennel bulb, stalks trimmed & bulb cut lengthwise into ¼-inch-thick slivers

1 red onion, sliced crosswise into ¼-inch-thick rings

½ cup apple cider

¼ cup sherry vinegar

⅓ cup Calamata or other brine-cured olives, pitted

1 tablespoon minced fresh oregano or 1 teaspoon dried

Salt & freshly ground black pepper to taste

1 pound fresh Cracked Black Pepper Linguine (p. 15) or dried linguine

4 ounces Asiago cheese, thinly shaved

3 tablespoons coarsely chopped fresh flat-leaf parsley

Sprigs of fresh oregano, for garnish (optional)

Linguine with Fennel, Olives
& Shaved Asiago (overleaf)

TAGLIATELLE WITH GRILLED VEGETABLES & PARMESAN

SERVES 6

IT IS NOT NECESSARY IN THIS RECIPE TO GRILL EACH PIECE
OF EGGPLANT, ZUCCHINI, OR ONION UNTIL IT IS COOKED COMPLETELY
THROUGH. SQUEEZE THE FRESH LEMON JUICE OVER THE
VEGETABLES AS SOON THEY COME OFF THE GRILL SO THEY WILL
ABSORB THE FRESH LEMON FLAVOR AND REMAIN MOIST.

P repare the grill. In a large bowl, drizzle ¼ cup of the oil over the garlic, rosemary, hot pepper flakes, and the salt and pepper, and stir to coat. Add the eggplant, zucchini, bell peppers, onion, and mushrooms, and stir to coat.

Grill the eggplant, zucchini, peppers, and onions over medium-hot coals for about 3 minutes on each side, the mushrooms for 1 to 2 minutes, or until all the vegetables are just slightly softened. Cool the mixture slightly.

Working quickly, halve or quarter the mushrooms, depending on the size, and return to the bowl. Cut the remaining vegetables into 1- to 1½-inch triangular shapes or chunks and add to the bowl. Add the lemon juice and parsley and toss gently to combine. Cover the vegetables to keep them warm.

Meanwhile, cook the pasta following the basic method (p. 13) until al dente. Drain well.

In a large skillet, heat the remaining 2 tablespoons oil over medium heat. Add the pasta and vegetables and toss until heated through and well combined. Divide among heated bowls and serve immediately, passing lemon wedges, Parmesan, and olive oil.

¼ cup plus 2 tablespoons olive oil

2 garlic cloves, minced

1 tablespoon minced fresh rosemary

½ teaspoon hot pepper flakes

Salt & freshly ground black pepper to taste

½ eggplant, peeled if desired, cut lengthwise into ¼-inch-thick slices

1 zucchini, cut into ½-inch slices

1 red bell pepper, cored, seeded & quartered

½ green bell pepper, cored, seeded & halved

½ medium-size red onion, cut into ½-inch slices

3 portobello or 10 medium-size mushrooms

Juice of 1 lemon

2 tablespoons coarsely chopped fresh flat-leaf parsley

1 pound fresh tagliatelle (p. 12) or dried tagliatelle

Lemon wedges, freshly shaved Parmesan cheese & olive oil

FETTUCCINE WITH
WINTER VEGETABLES

SERVES 4 TO 6

THE TRADITIONAL EASTERN EUROPEAN COMBINATION
OF CABBAGE, POTATOES, AND CARAWAY SEEDS IS A GOOD COMPLEMENT
FOR THE NUTTY, SOMEWHAT SWEET TASTE OF WHOLE-
WHEAT PASTA. USE THE LEFTOVER ROASTED GARLIC SPREAD ON
CRUSTY BREAD OR IN SOUP.

ROASTED GARLIC

1 whole head garlic

2 teaspoons olive oil

2 medium-size baking potatoes,
  unpeeled, halved lengthwise
  & sliced crosswise into
  ¼-inch-thick slices

4 tablespoons (½ stick) butter

1 onion, in ¼-inch-thick slices

4 cups very thinly sliced Napa
  or Savoy cabbage

¼ teaspoon caraway seeds

¾ cup chicken broth or
  vegetable broth

½ cup dry white wine

1 teaspoon Dijon mustard

2 tablespoons minced fresh parsley

Salt & freshly ground black
  pepper to taste

12 ounces fresh or dried
  whole-wheat fettuccine

4 to 6 ounces aged white Cheddar,
  smoked Cheddar, or Gruyère
  cheese, thinly shaved

Sprigs of fresh dill, for garnish

Roast the garlic: Preheat the oven to 375°F. Place the garlic in a small baking dish and drizzle with the oil. Cover with foil and bake for 25 to 35 minutes, or until the cloves feel soft. Pull 2 cloves from the head, squeeze the soft pulp from the skins, and set aside. Squeeze the pulp from the remaining cloves and refrigerate for up to 3 days.

Meanwhile, in a large pot of lightly salted boiling water, cook the potatoes for 6 to 10 minutes, or until just tender. Drain, rinse under cold running water to stop the cooking, and set aside.

In a large nonreactive skillet, melt the butter over medium heat. Add the reserved roasted garlic and the onion and cook for 1 to 2 minutes, or until the onion begins to soften. Stir in the cabbage and caraway seeds, add the broth and wine, and cook, covered, for 1 to 2 minutes, or until the cabbage begins to wilt. Stir in the potatoes and mustard and cook, uncovered, for 6 to 8 minutes, or until the vegetables are tender but not mushy. Remove from the heat, stir in the parsley, and season with salt and pepper.

Meanwhile, cook the pasta following the basic method (p. 13) until al dente. Drain, reserving 1 cup of the water.

In a large bowl, gently toss together the pasta and cabbage mixture. Add the reserved cooking water if the mixture seems dry. Serve immediately, garnished with the cheese and the dill sprigs.

CAPELLINI WITH GRILLED PORTOBELLO MUSHROOMS

SERVES 4 TO 6

PORTOBELLO MUSHROOMS HAVE A RICH,

WOODSY FLAVOR THAT BLENDS WELL WITH ROASTED GARLIC

AND THYME. IF PORTOBELLOS ARE NOT AVAILABLE,

FRESH SHIITAKES ARE THE BEST SUBSTITUTE, BUT EVEN GRILLED

WHITE MUSHROOMS WOULD BE DELICIOUS.

¼ cup extra-virgin olive oil

3 tablespoons mashed Roasted
    Garlic (p. 38)

2 tablespoons minced fresh thyme

4 large portobello mushrooms
    (3 to 4 ounces each), stemmed

½ cup olive oil

1 pound dried capellini

Sprigs of fresh thyme or fresh
    flat-leaf parsley, for garnish

Freshly grated Parmesan cheese
    (optional)

Prepare a grill or preheat the broiler, with the pan 4 inches from the heat source.

In a large skillet, heat the extra-virgin olive oil with the garlic and thyme over medium heat until hot but not smoking. Remove the skillet from the heat and let the mixture steep while you grill the mushrooms and prepare the pasta.

Brush the mushroom caps generously on both sides with ½ cup olive oil. Grill or broil the mushrooms for about 2 to 3 minutes on each side, or until they are sizzling, slightly softened, and browned, but the centers are firm. Remove them from the heat and set aside.

Cook the pasta following the basic method (p. 13) until al dente. Drain well.

Meanwhile, slice the mushroom caps into ¼-inch-thick slices.

Return the pasta to the cooking pot, add the flavored oil, and toss to coat. If necessary, quickly reheat the pasta over high heat. Divide the pasta among heated bowls and arrange the mushroom slices on top. Garnish with the thyme or parsley. Serve immediately, and pass Parmesan if desired.

CHINESE EGG NOODLES WITH
SPICY SHREDDED VEGETABLES

SERVES 6

THE TINY SLIVERS OF CARROT, RED BELL PEPPER AND

SNOWPEAS COOK IN LESS THAN A MINUTE, SO COOK THE NOODLES

FIRST AND THEN THE VEGETABLES. THE CHILE OIL SHOULD

NEVER BE USED FOR COOKING AS OVERHEATING IT CAUSES IT TO

TASTE BITTER AND UNPLEASANT. USE SPARINGLY; IT IS HOT.

Prepare the infused oil: In a small nonreactive saucepan, heat the peanut oil and sesame oil over medium heat. Add the chile powder or pepper flakes; they should sizzle, but not brown or burn. Cook for about 30 seconds, then remove from the heat. Strain the oil through a fine-mesh sieve or cheesecloth, set aside, and discard the solids.

Cook the noodles or pasta following the basic method (p. 13) until al dente. Drain well, rinse, and drain again. Set aside.

Meanwhile, in a large nonreactive skillet, heat the peanut oil over medium-high heat. Add the ginger and garlic and cook for 30 seconds. Add the carrots, snow peas, bell pepper, and green onions. Stir quickly to evenly combine the vegetables and continue to stir for 30 to 45 seconds. Add the noodles to the vegetable mixture. Stir in the soy sauce, rice vinegar, and 3 to 4 tablespoons of the chile oil. Divide the noodles and vegetables among heated serving bowls and serve immediately.

CHILE-INFUSED OIL

¼ cup peanut oil

1 teaspoon Oriental sesame oil

½ teaspoon Chinese red chile powder or hot pepper flakes

1 pound fresh Chinese egg noodles or any long dried pasta, such as spaghetti or linguine

2 tablespoons peanut oil

3 tablespoons grated peeled fresh ginger

2 garlic cloves, minced

3 cups shredded carrots

3 cups snow peas, thinly sliced

1 medium-size red bell pepper, cored, seeded & cut into 2- by ¼-inch sticks

3 green onions, sliced

2 tablespoons soy sauce

¼ cup rice vinegar

SPAGHETTINI WITH
MIDDLE-EASTERN MEATBALLS

SERVES 6

THESE MIDDLE-EASTERN SPICED MEATBALLS IN A
CINNAMON SCENTED SAUCE ARE SURPRISINGLY SIMPLE TO MAKE.
ADD A SPINACH SALAD STREWN WITH POMEGRANATE
SEEDS AND ORANGE SEGMENTS, SOME CRUSTY SOURDOUGH BREAD,
A GLASS OF RED WINE; AND DINNER IS COMPLETE.

MEATBALLS

1½ pounds ground turkey

½ onion, finely chopped

¾ cup fresh bread crumbs

⅓ cup dried currants or seedless
dark raisins, finely chopped

2 garlic cloves, minced

¼ teaspoon fennel seeds

⅛ teaspoon cumin seeds

2 tablespoons minced fresh
flat-leaf parsley

3 tablespoons olive oil

SWEET-AND-SPICY SAUCE

2 tablespoons butter

2 tablespoons olive oil

½ onion, finely chopped

1 small red or green bell pepper,
cored, seeded & finely
chopped

2 garlic cloves, minced

¼ cup dry red wine

1 (28-ounce) can peeled whole
tomatoes in juice

2 teaspoons honey

1 teaspoon hot pepper flakes

¼ teaspoon ground cinnamon

2 teaspoons minced fresh rosemary
or ¼ teaspoon dried

Prepare the meatballs: In a large bowl, combine all the ingredients and mix well with your hands. Pull off small pieces of the mixture and roll into 1½- to 2-inch balls; you should have about 2½ dozen.

In a large nonstick skillet, heat the oil over medium heat. Working in batches, add the meatballs and cook, turning frequently, for about 10 minutes, or until browned on all sides, adding more oil if necessary. Transfer to a platter.

Prepare the tomato sauce: In the same skillet, melt the butter with the oil over medium heat. Add the chopped onion, bell pepper, and garlic and cook, stirring frequently, for 5 to 7 minutes, or until the vegetables are softened. Stir in the red wine, scraping up any browned bits from the bottom of the skillet. Reduce the heat to medium-low and add the tomatoes with their juice, the honey, hot pepper flakes, ground cinnamon, rosemary, oregano, and parsley. Cook, partially covered, stirring occasionally to break up the tomatoes, for about 20 minutes to blend the flavors. Season with the salt and pepper. Add the meatballs to the sauce and rewarm them, about 10 minutes.

Meanwhile, cook the pasta following the basic method (p. 13) until al dente. Drain well.

Divide the pasta among heated serving bowls and top with the meatballs and sauce. Top the meatballs with the cheese and sprinkle with mint leaves if desired. Serve immediately.

VARIATION

• Freshly ground beef, veal, and pork can all be substituted for the turkey in these meatballs, either on their own or in combination.

2 teaspoons minced fresh oregano
or ¼ teaspoon dried

2 teaspoons chopped fresh
flat-leaf parsley

Salt & freshly ground black
pepper to taste

1 pound dried or fresh spaghettini

6 ounces feta cheese, crumbled

Fresh mint leaves, thinly slivered

RED PEPPER FETTUCCINE WITH GRILLED CHICKEN & LIME

SERVES 4 TO 6

THIS PASTA WAS INSPIRED BY THE FLAVORS
OF FAJITAS, WARM TORTILLAS FILLED WITH STRIPS OF SPICED
GRILLED MEAT. BE CAREFUL NOT TO OVERCOOK
THE CHICKEN AT THE BEGINNING, AS IT WILL CONTINUE TO
COOK LATER WHEN IT IS ADDED TO THE CORN.

3 boneless skinless chicken breast
halves (about 3 ounces each)

2 tablespoons butter

2 garlic cloves, minced

¼ teaspoon cumin seeds

2 cups fresh or frozen corn
kernels (about 8 ounces)

½ cup chicken broth

2 green onions, coarsely chopped

3 tablespoons coarsely chopped
fresh flat-leaf parsley

2 tablespoons coarsely chopped
fresh cilantro

Juice of 2 limes

1 pound fresh Red Pepper
Fettuccine (p. 13)
or dried fettuccine

2 cups Roasted Tomato Sauce
(p. 24)

Sprigs of fresh flat-leaf parsley,
for garnish

Prepare a grill or preheat the broiler, with the pan 4 to 6 inches from the heat source.

Grill or broil the chicken for 2 to 3 minutes per side, or until no longer pink in the center. Cut the chicken lengthwise into 2-inch-long strips, about ¼ inch wide, and set aside.

In a large nonreactive skillet, melt the butter over medium heat. Add the garlic and cumin seeds and cook for 30 seconds. Add the corn and chicken broth and cook, stirring frequently, for 2 to 3 minutes. Add the cooked chicken, green onions, parsley, and cilantro and cook for 1 to 2 minutes, or until heated through. Remove the skillet from the heat and stir in the lime juice.

Meanwhile, cook the pasta following the basic method (p. 13) until al dente. Drain well.

While the pasta cooks, heat the tomato sauce in a small nonreactive skillet.

Return the pasta to the pot and add the chicken-corn mixture, tossing gently to mix. Divide among heated serving bowls. Drizzle the tomato sauce over each serving, garnish with sprigs of parsley, and serve immediately.

CHICKEN & BROCCOLI WITH
NOODLES & THAI PEANUT SAUCE

SERVES 4 TO 6

THIS THAI PEANUT SAUCE IS MEDIUM-HOT,

BUT YOU MAY CONTROL THE DEGREE OF SPICINESS

BY INCREASING OR DECREASING THE

AMOUNT OF CHILE OIL OR HOT PEPPER FLAKES.

I n a large pot of boiling water, blanch the broccoli florets for about 2 minutes, or until bright green and crisp-tender. Drain, plunge into a bowl of ice water, and drain.

In a large nonreactive skillet, melt 1½ tablespoons of the butter over medium-high heat. Add half the chicken and cook, stirring frequently, for 3 to 5 minutes, or until cooked through. Transfer to a paper-towel-lined platter, and cook the remaining chicken in the remaining butter.

Add the coconut milk, broth, peanut butter, vinegar, lime juice, garlic, and oil to the skillet and bring to a simmer, stirring until smooth. Stir in the chicken, broccoli, green onions, and peanuts and heat through. Remove from the heat.

Meanwhile, cook the lo mein noodles or pasta following the basic method (p. 13), until al dente. Drain well. Toss the noodles with the sauce in the skillet. Divide among heated serving bowls and garnish with the cilantro and lime wedges.

4 cups broccoli florets

3 tablespoons butter

3 boneless, skinless chicken breast halves, (about 3 ounces each), cut into long strips ½ inch wide

1 cup canned unsweetened coconut milk

¾ cup chicken broth

⅓ cup peanut butter

2 tablespoons cider vinegar

2 to 3 tablespoons fresh lime juice

4 garlic cloves, minced

1 teaspoon hot Chile-Infused Oil (p. 43) or 1 teaspoon hot pepper flakes

3 green onions, chopped

½ cup unsalted dry-roasted peanuts

1 pound fresh lo mein noodles or 1 pound long dried pasta, such as fettuccine

¼ cup chopped fresh cilantro

Lime wedges, for garnish

RIGATONI WITH
BOLOGNESE SAUCE

SERVES 4 TO 6

OPINIONS DIFFER ON WHAT DEFINES THE
AUTHENTIC BOLOGNESE SAUCE. SOME INSIST ON
WHITE WINE, OTHERS ADD A TOUCH OF
MILK. THIS VERSION REQUIRES MUCH LESS SIMMERING
THAN THE CLASSIC BOLOGNESE.

1 carrot, roughly chopped

1 celery stalk, roughly chopped

1 onion, roughly chopped

5 medium-size mushrooms,
   stemmed & cut up

3 garlic cloves

¼ cup olive oil

1 (1½-pound) mixture of ground
   veal, beef, and pork or all
   ground beef or ground turkey

1 cup dry red wine

1 (28-ounce) can crushed
   tomatoes in juice

1 bay leaf

1 sprig fresh rosemary or
   ½ teaspoon dried

1 sprig fresh thyme or
   ½ teaspoon dried

1 sprig fresh oregano or
   ½ teaspoon dried

Salt & freshly ground black
   pepper to taste

1 pound dried rigatoni

¼ cup chopped fresh
   flat-leaf parsley

Freshly grated Parmesan cheese

In a food processor fitted with the metal blade, combine the carrot, celery, onion, mushrooms, and garlic and process until finely chopped.

In a large nonreactive skillet, heat the oil over medium-high heat. Add the chopped vegetables and cook, stirring often, for 4 to 6 minutes, or until softened. Add the ground meat and cook, stirring frequently, for 8 to 10 minutes, or until the meat is no longer pink. Add the wine, reduce the heat to medium, and stir in the tomatoes with their juice.

Using kitchen string, tie the bay leaf and herb sprigs together and add the herb bundle to the sauce, or add the bay leaf and dried herbs. Reduce the heat to low and simmer, stirring occasionally, for 20 minutes, or until the sauce is thickened. Season with the salt and pepper and remove the herb bundle. Keep warm. (The sauce can be refrigerated, tightly covered, for up to five days.)

Meanwhile, cook the pasta following the basic method (p. 13) until al dente. Drain well.

Divide the pasta among heated serving bowls. Top each with Bolognese sauce, garnish with parsley, and serve, passing the Parmesan.

LINGUINE WITH HAM & PEAS IN ROASTED GARLIC CREAM SAUCE

SERVES 4

CREAM-BASED SAUCES DON'T HAVE
TO BE HEAVY, AS THIS RECIPE DEMONSTRATES.
THE USUAL HEAVY CREAM HAS BEEN
REPLACED IN PART WITH CHICKEN BROTH AND
WHITE WINE TO MAKE A LIGHTER SAUCE.

Prepare the garlic cream sauce: In a large non-reactive skillet, heat the butter over medium heat. Add the onion and roasted garlic and cook, stirring, for 1 to 2 minutes, or until the onion is softened. Add the ham, peas, broth, wine, cream, and half-and-half. Increase the heat to high and bring to a simmer. Cook, stirring often, for 2 to 3 minutes, or until the sauce is reduced and thickened. Remove the skillet from the heat.

Meanwhile, cook the pasta following the basic method (p. 13) until al dente. Drain well, reserving a little of the cooking water.

Add the pasta to the sauce, return the skillet to medium-high heat, and gently toss the pasta and sauce together until well mixed and heated through. If the sauce seems dry, add a splash or two of the reserved cooking water. Divide the pasta among heated pasta bowls, top with sage, and serve.

ROASTED GARLIC CREAM SAUCE

2 tablespoons butter

½ onion, very thinly sliced

¼ cup mashed Roasted Garlic, (p. 38)

8 ounces thinly sliced good-quality smoked ham or 6 ounces thinly sliced prosciutto, cut into ¼-inch julienne

2 cups frozen tiny green peas

¼ cup chicken broth

¼ cup dry white wine

1 cup heavy cream

½ cup half-and-half

12 ounces fresh or dried linguine

Chopped fresh sage, for garnish

FUSILLI WITH BROCCOLI RABE & SWEET SAUSAGE

SERVES 4

SLIGHTLY BITTER-FLAVORED BROCCOLI RABE, ALSO CALLED
BROCCOLI RAAB OR BROCCOLETTI DI RAPE, IS NOT PART OF THE BROCCOLI
PLANT AT ALL, BUT ACTUALLY THE LEAFY GREENS OF A
TYPE OF TURNIP. KALE IS THE BEST SUBSTITUTE, BUT MUSTARD GREENS
AND ESCAROLE ARE FINE ALTERNATIVES.

In a large nonreactive skillet, cook the sausage over medium heat, breaking up the meat with a wooden spoon, for 8 to 10 minutes, or until no longer pink. Transfer the meat to a paper-towel-lined plate to drain. Wipe out the skillet.

In the same skillet, heat the oil over medium-high heat. Add the onion and cook for 30 to 45 seconds, or until it begins to soften. Add the garlic and cook for 1 minute. Stir in the broccoli rabe and sausage and cook until the broccoli rabe begins to sizzle. Add the broth and wine, cover tightly, and cook for 2 to 3 minutes, or until the leaves are wilted and the stalks are crisp-tender. Remove the skillet from the heat.

Meanwhile, cook the pasta following the basic method (p. 13) until al dente. Drain well.

Add the pasta to the sausage mixture, return the skillet to medium-high heat, and toss the pasta and sauce together until well combined and heated through. Divide among heated serving bowls and serve with lemon wedges and Parmesan.

1 pound sweet Italian sausage
or sausage links with
casings removed

¼ cup olive oil

1 onion, thinly sliced

4 garlic cloves, thinly sliced

8 cups loosely packed stemmed
& coarsely chopped broccoli
rabe (1 large bunch)

½ cup chicken broth

¼ cup dry white wine

12 ounces dried fusilli

Lemon wedges

Freshly grated Parmesan cheese

SESAME ORANGE BEEF WITH FRIED CELLOPHANE NOODLES

SERVES 4

CELLOPHANE NOODLES, ALSO CALLED GLASS NOODLES OR

BEAN THREADS (AFTER THE MUNG BEANS FROM WHICH THEY ARE MADE),

ARE THIN, WHITISH STRANDS SOLD COILED IN PLASTIC PACKAGES.

WHEN FRIED, THEY ALMOST INSTANTLY INCREASE THREE TO FOUR TIMES

IN VOLUME, SO JUST 2 OUNCES IS ENOUGH TO SERVE FOUR.

SESAME ORANGE MARINADE

3 tablespoons rice vinegar

2 teaspoons Oriental sesame oil

Grated zest & juice of 1 orange

2 garlic cloves, minced

1 tablespoon grated peeled
    fresh ginger

¼ teaspoon Chinese red chile
    powder or hot pepper flakes

1¼ pounds top sirloin steak

3½ cups broccoli florets

2 tablespoons sesame seeds

NOODLES

Vegetable oil, for deep-frying

2 ounces cellophane noodles or
    bean threads

2 tablespoons olive oil

3 cups sliced shiitake or
    white mushrooms, stemmed

1 (7-ounce) can whole baby corn,
    drained & rinsed

1 (5-ounce) can sliced water
    chestnuts, drained & rinsed

⅓ cup tamari or soy sauce

Prepare the marinade: In a medium-size nonreactive bowl, whisk together all the ingredients. Set aside.

Cut the steak into thin strips about 4 inches long and ¼ inch thick. Add to the marinade, stirring to coat. Cover and refrigerate for at least 1 hour or overnight.

In a large saucepan of boiling water, blanch the broccoli for about 1 minute, or until barely crisp-tender. Drain, plunge into ice water to stop the cooking, drain again and set aside.

In a small skillet, toast the sesame seeds over medium-high heat, stirring often, for 2 to 3 minutes, or until lightly browned and aromatic. Transfer the seeds to a small plate.

Prepare the noodles: Pour enough oil into a wok or large heavy skillet to reach a depth of 1½ to 2 inches and heat until very hot. (The oil is hot enough when a single noodle placed in the oil immediately puffs and crisps.) Separate the noodles into 4 portions, pulling the noodles apart from each other over a large bowl, as they tend to fly about. Using a skimmer or slotted spoon, fry the portions of noodles one at a time for 2 or 3 seconds on each side, or until puffed. Transfer to a paper towel-lined platter or baking sheet and set aside. Drain the vegetable oil from the wok.

In the same wok or skillet, heat the olive oil over medium-high heat. Add the mushrooms and cook for about 2 minutes, or until lightly browned but slightly undercooked. Transfer to a small bowl.

Drain the beef strips, reserving the marinade, and add the beef to the wok. Cook, stirring frequently, for 2 to 3 minutes, or until lightly browned. Stir in the broccoli, mushrooms, baby corn, and water chestnuts. Add the reserved marinade and the tamari or soy sauce and cook for about 2 minutes or until the sauce is bubbly and the vegetables are heated through.

Pile the fried noodles on a warmed serving platter to make a nest. Arrange the beef and vegetables in the center and sprinkle the toasted sesame seeds over all. Serve immediately.

PASTA ALLA CARBONARA

THERE ARE MANY VERSIONS OF PASTA CARBONARA, THE
HEAVIEST HAVING LOTS OF EGGS AS WELL AS HEAVY CREAM. FOR A
LEANER DISH STILL, USE ONLY 1 EGG, 4 OUNCES PANCETTA,
1 CUP OF WINE, AND 1 TABLESPOON CHEESE. THE EGGS ARE ADDED
RAW AND COOKED BY THE HEAT OF THE PASTA.

2 large eggs

¼ cup freshly grated
    Parmesan cheese

¼ cup chopped fresh
    flat-leaf parsley

6 ounces chopped pancetta
    or bacon

1 cup julienned red bell pepper

⅔ cup dry white wine

12 ounces fresh or dried spaghetti,
    linguine, or fettuccine

½ teaspoon freshly ground
    black pepper

Salt to taste

In a small bowl, whisk together the eggs, Parmesan, and parsley. Set aside.

In a large nonreactive skillet, cook the pancetta or bacon over medium-low heat, stirring often, for about 10 minutes, or until browned and beginning to crisp. Drain off all but about 1 tablespoon of the fat from the pan. Increase the heat to medium-high and add the bell pepper. Cook, stirring frequently, for 1 to 2 minutes, or until the pepper is just softened. Add the white wine and simmer for 30 to 45 seconds. Remove the skillet from the heat.

Meanwhile, cook the pasta following the basic method (p. 13) until al dente. Drain well.

Add the pasta to the pancetta or bacon in the skillet, stirring to mix well. Add the egg mixture and black pepper and quickly toss together until well combined. Season with the salt, depending on the saltiness of the pancetta or bacon. Transfer the hot pasta to a large heated serving bowl or heated bowls and serve immediately.

PAPPARDELLE WITH FRESH TUNA, CAPERS & OLIVES

SERVES 4

PAPPARADELLE IS, REALLY, THE EASIEST OF ALL PASTAS TO MAKE
BY HAND: IT IS SIMPLY 5 TO 6 INCH LONG RIBBONS CUT ¾ TO 1 INCH
WIDE. THIS SAUCE IS WELL SUITED TO THESE BROAD NOODLES
BECAUSE IT HAS A BROTH-LIKE CONSISTENCY. OTHER PASTA SHAPES HAVE
A TENDENCY TO BECOME SOGGY WHEN SERVED IN THIS MANNER.

In a large nonreactive skillet, heat the oil over medium-high heat. Add the onion and cook, stirring frequently, for 1 to 2 minutes, or until the onion begins to soften slightly. Add the garlic and the ginger, if desired. Cook, stirring, for 1 minute. Add the tuna and hot pepper flakes and cook, stirring frequently, for about 2 minutes, or until the tuna is lightly browned.

Stir in the broth or clam juice, wine, tomatoes, olives, and capers and bring to a boil. Reduce the heat to medium-low and simmer for 2 to 3 minutes. Stir in the balsamic vinegar and parsley and season with the salt and pepper. Remove the skillet from the heat.

Meanwhile, cook the pasta following the basic method (p. 13) until al dente. Drain well.

Divide the pasta among heated bowls, top with the sauce, and serve immediately.

3 tablespoons olive oil

½ onion, cut into
¼-inch-thick slivers

2 garlic cloves, thinly sliced

2 teaspoons grated peeled fresh
ginger (optional)

1 pound fresh tuna steak, cut into
¾- to 1-inch chunks

½ teaspoon hot pepper flakes

½ cup chicken broth or
bottled clam juice

¼ cup dry white wine

4 fresh ripe or canned plum
tomatoes, chopped, plus 2
tablespoons juice if using
canned

½ cup Calamata or other
brine-cured olives, pitted &
very coarsely chopped

1 tablespoon capers, rinsed &
drained

2 tablespoons balsamic vinegar

2 tablespoons chopped fresh
flat-leaf parsley

Salt & freshly ground black
pepper to taste

12 ounces fresh or dried
pappardelle or fettuccine

FETTUCCINE WITH
SMOKED SALMON & ENDIVE

SERVES 4 TO 6

BELGIAN ENDIVE IS USUALLY USED RAW IN SALADS,

OR OCCASIONALLY BRAISED IN BUTTER AND SERVED AS A VEGETABLE

SIDE DISH. HERE IT LENDS A SLIGHTLY SWEET CRUNCHINESS

TO THE SMOOTH, RICH SAUCE. WHEN CUT INTO A THIN JULIENNE, IT

MAKES A DELICATE FEATHERY GARNISH AS WELL.

2 tablespoons butter

4 to 5 ounces smoked salmon, coarsely chopped

1¼ cups snap peas, stemmed

¼ cup half-and-half

½ cup heavy cream

3 tablespoons snipped fresh dill

1 teaspoon brandy (optional)

1 head Belgian endive, trimmed, halved lengthwise & cut into ¼-inch julienne

Salt & freshly ground black pepper to taste

1 pound fresh or dried fettuccine

Sprigs of fresh dill & very thin endive julienne, for garnish

Prepare the sauce: In a large skillet, melt the butter over medium-high heat. Add the salmon, snap peas, half-and-half, heavy cream, and dill and bring to a boil, stirring often. Reduce the heat to medium, add the brandy if desired, and simmer for about 2 minutes, or until the sauce has thickened slightly. Add the endive and cook for about 30 to 45 seconds, or until the endive has wilted but is still crisp. Remove the skillet from the heat.

Meanwhile, cook the pasta following the basic method (p. 13) until al dente. Drain well.

Add the pasta to the sauce and toss to mix well. Season with the salt and pepper. Divide the pasta among heated serving bowls, garnish with dill sprigs or endive julienne, and serve immediately.

VARIATIONS

• Substitute 1 cup frozen tiny green peas for the snap peas.

• Substitute 1 cup julienned leeks for the endive. Sauté the leeks in the butter for 1 minute before adding the salmon.

• Substitute 1 small fennel bulb for the endive. Cut it into ⅛- to ¼-inch-thick slivers and sauté in the butter for 1 minute before adding the salmon.

SEAFOOD & LINGUINE IN RED CURRY BROTH

SERVES 4 TO 6

THE COMPLEX HEAT OF THIS SAUCE DERIVES FROM
RED CURRY PASTE, WHICH IS A MIXTURE OF GROUND HOT RED CHILES,
GARLIC, ONION, AND OTHER SPICES
INCLUDING CORIANDER SEEDS AND LEMON GRASS. THE PASTE IS
AVAILABLE IN SPECIALTY AND ASIAN MARKETS.

In a large nonreactive skillet, melt the butter over medium-high heat. Add the onion and garlic and cook, stirring occasionally, without browning, for about 1 to 2 minutes, or until the onion begins to soften. Stir in the bell peppers, and cook for 1 to 2 minutes, or until the peppers just begins to soften. Add the shrimp and scallops and cook, stirring, for about 2 minutes, or until the shrimp begin to turn pink and the scallops are no longer translucent.

Add the wine and clam juice, and reduce the heat to medium. Stir in the tomato paste, curry paste, the curry powder, if desired, and the tomatoes. Add the mussels and clams. Cook for 3 to 5 minutes, or until the mussels and clams open. Discard any unopened shellfish. Stir in the basil, parsley, and cilantro and remove from the heat. Season with the pepper.

Meanwhile, cook the pasta following the basic method (p. 13) until al dente. Drain well.

Divide the hot pasta among heated serving bowls and top with the seafood and broth. Serve immediately.

3 tablespoons butter

1 onion, halved lengthwise & cut into ¼-inch-thick slivers

3 garlic cloves, very thinly sliced

1 each green and red or yellow bell pepper, cored, seeded & cut into ¼-inch-wide slices

½ pound large shrimp, peeled & deveined

½ pound bay scallops

½ cup dry white wine

1 (8-ounce) bottle clam juice

2 tablespoons tomato paste

2 teaspoons red curry paste

1 teaspoon curry powder (optional)

2 cups chopped fresh or canned tomatoes

¾ pound mussels, scrubbed & debearded

1 pound cherrystone clams, scrubbed

3 tablespoons minced fresh basil

3 tablespoons minced fresh flat-leaf parsley

2 tablespoons minced fresh cilantro

¼ teaspoon freshly ground black pepper

1 pound fresh or dried linguine

PUMPKIN-CHIPOTLE RAVIOLI IN A SPICY PUMPKIN SAUCE

A CLASSIC AUTUMN DISH, THESE RAVIOLI ARE

OFTEN SERVED AS A FIRST COURSE IN A SIMPLE CHICKEN BROTH

OR WITH MELTED BUTTER AND FRESHLY GRATED

PARMESAN CHEESE. THE UNUSUAL SAUCE IN OUR VERSION IS

SPICED WITH CHIPOTLES, OR SMOKED JALAPEÑOS

PUMPKIN-CHIPOTLE FILLING

2 tablespoons olive oil

½ cup finely chopped onion

1 garlic clove, minced

2 cups canned pumpkin purée

2 tablespoons freshly grated Parmesan cheese

1 chipotle chile in adobo sauce, finely chopped

1 tablespoon minced fresh cilantro

RAVIOLI

½ recipe Egg Pasta with machine (p. 12) or 1 recipe Egg Pasta by hand (p. 14), extruded or rolled into 6 sheets, 5 to 6 inches wide, 12 to 14 inches long & no more than ¹/₁₆ inch thick

1 large egg, lightly beaten

Prepare the filling: In a medium-size skillet, heat the oil over medium heat. Add the onion and garlic and cook, stirring frequently, for 1 to 2 minutes, or until the onion begins to soften. Stir in the pumpkin and Parmesan cheese and remove from the heat. Stir in the chipotle chile and cilantro. Transfer the filling to a bowl, reserving ½ cup filling for the sauce in another bowl.

Prepare the ravioli: Place a sheet of pasta dough on a lightly floured work surface. In 2 parallel rows, running the length of the sheet, mound generous teaspoons of the filling, spacing the mounds 2 inches apart, creating 10 to 12 mounds. Using a pastry brush, moisten a second sheet of the dough with the beaten egg. Place the pasta, moistened side down, on the first and press the top sheet of pasta down onto the bottom sheet, pressing around the mounds of filling to seal. Using a paring knife or pizza cutter, cut into square ravioli and press the edges again to seal. Continue to make ravioli with the remaining filling and remaining pasta. Place the ravioli between sheets of waxed paper on baking sheets and place in the freezer until ready to cook. (Chilling the ravioli helps them to keep their shape when cooked and helps to prevent seams from opening.)

Prepare the sauce: In a small skillet, melt the butter over medium heat. Add the garlic and cook,

stirring, for 30 to 45 seconds, or until aromatic. Stir in the wine, half-and-half, cream, and the reserved pumpkin filling, reduce the heat, and simmer, whisking often, for 3 to 5 minutes, or until the sauce has thickened enough to coat the back of a spoon. Remove from the heat, stir in the chipotle, and set aside.

Cook the ravioli following the basic method (p. 13) for 3 to 5 minutes, or until al dente, firm but tender. Drain well and divide among heated serving bowls or plates. Spoon the hot (reheated if necessary) sauce over the ravioli and dot the sauce with tiny flecks of adobo sauce if desired. Garnish with cilantro or parsley and serve immediately.

SPICY PUMPKIN SAUCE

2 tablespoons butter

1 garlic clove, minced

¼ cup dry white wine

1 cup half-and-half

½ cup heavy cream

½ cup reserved Pumpkin Filling (from above)

½ chipotle chile in adobo sauce, chopped

½ teaspoon adobo sauce from canned chipotles (optional)

Chopped fresh cilantro or flat-leaf parsley, for garnish

SWISS CHARD RAVIOLI IN ROASTED RED BELL PEPPER SAUCE

SWISS CHARD IS A FLAVORFUL ALTERNATIVE TO THE USUAL SPINACH FILLING. BE SURE TO SQUEEZE ALL THE EXCESS WATER FROM THE CHARD OR THE FILLING WILL BE WATERY AND THE RAVIOLI WILL NOT SEAL PROPERLY.

FILLING

1 bunch red or Swiss chard, stemmed & chopped (4 to 6 cups)

2 tablespoons olive oil

¼ cup chopped onion

2 garlic cloves, minced

¾ cup ricotta cheese

¼ cup freshly grated Parmesan cheese

1 large egg

⅛ teaspoon grated nutmeg

Salt & freshly ground black pepper to taste

RAVIOLI

½ recipe Egg Pasta with machine (p. 12) or 1 recipe Egg Pasta by hand (p. 14), extruded or rolled into 6 sheets, 5 to 6 inches wide, 12 to 14 inches long & no more than 1/16 inch thick

1 large egg, lightly beaten

Roasted Red Bell Pepper Sauce (p. 20)

Freshly grated Parmesan cheese & chopped fresh basil, for garnish

In a large skillet, combine the Swiss chard and 2 to 3 tablespoons of water. Cover and cook over high heat for 1 to 2 minutes, or until the chard is just wilted and somewhat crunchy. Drain well, let cool, then squeeze out the excess moisture. Place the chard in a medium-size bowl.

In a small skillet, heat the oil over medium heat. Add the onion and garlic and cook, stirring, for 1 to 2 minutes, or until the onion begins to soften. Add the mixture to the Swiss chard along with the ricotta, Parmesan, egg, nutmeg, salt, and pepper, stirring to combine.

Fill the ravioli as directed on p. 62; cook following basic method (p. 13).

Prepare the Roasted Red Bell Pepper Sauce. Divide the hot cooked ravioli among warmed serving plates and spoon about ¼ cup heated pepper sauce, over each serving. Garnish with Parmesan and basil. Serve immediately.

CHICKEN & SUN-DRIED
TOMATO RAVIOLI

SEASON THIS BALSAMIC VINEGAR-ACCENTED FILLING
WITH SALT JUDICIOUSLY, SINCE SUN-DRIED TOMATOES VARY
IN THEIR DEGREE OF SALTINESS. TRY SERVING THESE
RAVIOLI WITH UNCOOKED FRESH TOMATO SAUCE (P. 22)
WITH FRESHLY GRATED PARMESAN CHEESE.

I In a medium-size skillet, melt half the butter over medium heat. Add the onion and garlic and cook, stirring, for 1 minute, or until the onion is slightly softened. Add the remaining butter, the chicken, sun-dried tomatoes, and rosemary and cook, stirring frequently, for 3 to 5 minutes, or until the chicken is no longer pink in the center. Transfer to a food processor fitted with the metal blade and process until finely chopped. Transfer the chicken mixture to a medium-size bowl.

Return the skillet to the heat. Pour the broth into the skillet and scrape up any browned bits from the bottom of the skillet. Add the broth mixture to the chicken mixture along with the Parmesan, ricotta, parsley, vinegar, salt, and pepper, stirring until well combined.

Fill the ravioli as directed on p. 62; cook following basic method (p. 13) and serve.

FILLING

4 tablespoons (½ stick) unsalted butter

½ cup chopped onion

3 garlic cloves, minced

2 boneless, skinless chicken breasts (about 6 ounces each), cut into 1-inch chunks

4 sun-dried tomatoes, packed in oil, chopped

1 tablespoon minced fresh rosemary or 1 teaspoon dried

½ cup chicken broth

½ cup freshly grated Parmesan cheese

½ cup ricotta cheese

¼ cup chopped fresh flat-leaf parsley

1 tablespoon balsamic vinegar

Salt & freshly ground black pepper to taste

RAVIOLI

½ recipe Egg Pasta with machine (p. 12) or 1 recipe Egg Pasta by hand (p. 14), extruded or rolled into 6 sheets, 5 to 6 inches wide, 12 to 14 inches long & no more than ¹⁄₁₆ inch thick

ARTICHOKE & MASCARPONE CANNELLONI

SERVES 4 TO 6

CANNELLONI ARE SQUARES OF PASTA ROLLED INTO
TUBES AND FILLED, AND ARE OFTEN SERVED AS A FIRST COURSE
RATHER THAN AS AN ENTREE. THIS VEGETARIAN VERSION
INVOLVES SEVERAL COMPONENTS, BUT THE SAUCES CAN BE MADE
AHEAD, AND THE FINAL DISH IS SPECTACULAR.

ARTICHOKE FILLING

2 (14-ounce) cans artichoke hearts, drained, rinsed & coarsely chopped

1 cup mascarpone

¼ cup freshly grated Parmesan cheese

2 large egg yolks

1 green onion, chopped

3 tablespoons chopped fresh basil

2 tablespoons chopped fresh flat-leaf parsley

1 teaspoon grated lemon zest

Juice of ½ lemon

¼ teaspoon salt

⅛ teaspoon freshly ground black pepper

½ recipe Egg Pasta with machine (p. 12) or 1 recipe Egg Pasta by hand (p. 14), extruded or rolled into 6 sheets, 5 to 6 inches wide, 12 to 14 inches long & 1/16 inch thick

Prepare the filling: In a medium-size bowl, combine all the ingredients and stir until well combined. Cover and refrigerate.

Using a paring knife, cut each pasta sheet into two 5-inch squares, trimming the sides, for a total of 12 squares. In a medium-size saucepan of boiling water, cook the pasta, 2 to 3 squares at a time, for 1 to 1½ minutes, or until soft and pliable. With a slotted spoon, carefully remove the squares and plunge them into a bowl of ice water to stop the cooking.

Prepare the béchamel sauce: In a medium-size saucepan, melt the butter over medium heat. Stir in the flour and cook, stirring, for 1 minute or until the mixture is bubbly and smooth. Gradually stir in the milk until well blended and smooth and cook, stirring, for 3 to 4 minutes, or until the sauce has thickened. Season with the nutmeg and salt and pepper, and remove from the heat.

Assemble and bake the cannelloni: Preheat the oven to 350°F. Lightly coat a 13- by 9-inch baking pan with olive oil.

Remove the pasta squares from the cold water 2 or 3 at a time and pat dry using a clean towel. Place 3 generous tablespoons of the filling down the center of each square and roll up into a fairly tight cylinder about 1½ inches thick. Place the cannelloni, seam side down, in the prepared baking pan.

Spread the béchamel sauce over the cannelloni. Bake the cannelloni for about 25 to 30 minutes, or until the sauce begins to bubble and turn golden brown at the edges of the pan and the cannelloni are heated through. Using about ¼ cup of the bell pepper sauce, drizzle bold lines of the sauce over the béchamel.

Meanwhile, in a small nonreactive saucepan, heat the remaining bell pepper sauce.

Using a metal spatula, transfer the cannelloni to heated serving plates. Spoon bell pepper sauce around them. Sprinkle with the Parmesan and/or chopped fresh herbs if desired and serve immediately.

VARIATION

• *Eggplant & Gorgonzola Cannelloni*: In a large sauté pan, heat ⅓ cup olive oil. Add 5 cups of peeled, diced eggplant (½ inch) and cook, stirring often for 2 to 3 minutes. Add 2 thinly sliced garlic cloves and continue to cook a minute or two longer, or until the eggplant is cooked.

Transfer the mixture to a large bowl. Stir in ¼ cup chopped fresh parsley, ¾ cup freshly grated Parmesan cheese, ½ cup toasted pine nuts, and 1¼ cups crumbled gorgonzola cheese. Season with salt and freshly ground black pepper to taste. Fill, assemble and bake the cannelloni as directed above, with the bechamel and roasted bell pepper sauces.

BÉCHAMEL SAUCE

2 tablespoons butter

2 tablespoons all-purpose flour

1½ cups milk

Pinch of grated nutmeg

Pinch each of salt and freshly
   ground black pepper

1 cup Roasted Red Bell Pepper
   Sauce (p. 20)

Freshly grated Parmesan cheese
   (optional)

Chopped fresh flat-leaf parsley or
   basil, for garnish (optional)

LASAGNE WITH
RICOTTA & GREENS

S E R V E S   6   T O   8

IN LATE-NINETEENTH-CENTURY ITALY, LASAGNE WAS A
LAYERING OF COOKED PASTA WITH A MEAT SAUCE, BUTTER, AND
CHEESE, SERVED, UNBAKED, AS A FIRST COURSE. FOR
A MORE INTENSE TASTE IN THIS MAIN-COURSE LASAGNE, USE
ONLY ESCAROLE OR BROCCOLI RABE.

TOMATO SAUCE

⅓ cup olive oil

¾ cup chopped onions

4 garlic cloves, minced

½ cup dry white wine

1 (32-ounce) can crushed
    tomatoes in juice

1 (6-ounce) can tomato paste

1 teaspoon sugar

2 teaspoons minced fresh rosemary

1 teaspoon minced fresh oregano

½ teaspoon hot pepper flakes
    (optional)

RICOTTA FILLING

10 ounces spinach, Swiss chard,
    escarole, or broccoli rabe or
    a combination, rinsed, dried
    & coarsely chopped

2 tablespoons olive oil

1 medium-size onion, chopped

2 garlic cloves, minced

2 cups ricotta cheese

2 large eggs, lightly beaten

¼ teaspoon grated nutmeg

6 sun-dried tomatoes (not oil-
    packed), plumped in hot
    water & chopped

¼ cup chopped fresh parsley

Prepare the sauce: In a large nonreactive skillet, heat the oil over medium-high heat. Add the onions and garlic and cook, stirring frequently, for 1 to 2 minutes, or until the onions begin to soften. Add the wine and reduce the heat to medium-low. Stir in the tomatoes and tomato paste, then add the sugar, rosemary, oregano, and hot pepper flakes if desired and bring to a simmer. Simmer for about 15 minutes or until thickened. Remove from the heat.

Prepare the filling: In a medium-size saucepan, combine the greens with ½ cup water. Cook, covered, over medium-high heat for 1 to 2 minutes, or until the greens are wilted but still crisp-tender. Drain well, let cool, then place in a sieve and squeeze out the excess water. Set aside.

In a small skillet, heat the oil over medium-high heat. Add the onion and garlic and cook, stirring frequently, for 1 to 2 minutes, or until the onion begins to soften. Remove from the heat.

In a large bowl, combine the greens, onion and garlic, ricotta cheese, eggs, nutmeg, sun-dried tomatoes, parsley, basil, and Parmesan cheese and stir until well mixed. Season with the salt and pepper.

Assemble the lasagne: Preheat the oven to 350°F. Generously butter or oil a 13- by 9-inch baking pan.

Cook the lasagne noodles following the basic method (p. 13), or according to the package directions until al dente, firm but tender. Drain well.

Cover the bottom of the prepared pan with 4 lasagne noodles. Top with half the filling, a third of the sauce, and a third of the mozzarella cheese. Cover with 4 more lasagne noodles, the remaining filling, half of the remaining sauce, and half the remaining mozzarella cheese. Cover with the remaining 4 noodles, the remaining sauce and mozzarella cheese. Sprinkle the Parmesan cheese over the top.

Bake for 35 to 45 minutes, or until the lasagne is bubbly and browned around the edges. Let stand for 10 minutes before slicing and serving.

¼ cup minced fresh basil

½ cup freshly grated Parmesan cheese

¼ teaspoon salt

¼ teaspoon freshly ground black pepper

12 fresh or dried lasagne noodles (12 ounces)

3 cups shredded mozzarella cheese

½ cup freshly grated Parmesan cheese

CHICKEN LASAGNE
WITH CALABACITAS

SERVES 6 TO 8

CALABACITAS, WHICH MEANS "LITTLE SQUASH,"
HAS COME TO REFER TO A NEW MEXICAN DISH MADE
WITH GRATED ZUCCHINI AND YELLOW SQUASH,
CORN, GREEN CHILES, AND A TOUCH OF CREAM OR
SHREDDED CHEESE.

BÉCHAMEL SAUCE

4 tablespoons (½ stick) butter

½ teaspoon minced garlic

⅓ cup all-purpose flour

3 cups milk

⅛ teaspoon grated nutmeg

CALABACITAS

2 tablespoons butter

¾ cup chopped onions

3 cups shredded zucchini

3 cups shredded yellow squash

3 cups fresh or thawed
frozen corn kernels

¾ cup half-and-half

½ to ¾ cup chopped, roasted,
cored, peeled & seeded fresh
New Mexican or hatch green
chile peppers, or chopped
canned green chile peppers

Salt & freshly ground black
pepper to taste

Prepare the béchamel sauce: In a medium-size saucepan, melt the butter over medium heat. Add the garlic and cook, stirring, for 30 seconds. Stir in the flour and cook, stirring, for 1 minute, or until the mixture is bubbly and smooth. Gradually stir in the milk until well blended and smooth. Cook, stirring frequently, for 3 to 4 minutes, or until the sauce has thickened; cover the pan, and set aside.

Prepare the calabacitas: In a large skillet, melt the butter over medium-high heat. Add the onions and cook, stirring often, for 1 to 2 minutes, or until the onions begin to soften. Stir in the zucchini, yellow squash, and corn and cook, stirring frequently, for 2 to 3 minutes, or until the vegetables are crisp-tender. Stir in the half-and-half and green chiles. Season with salt and pepper. Remove from the heat and set aside.

Preheat the oven to 350°F. Generously butter or oil a 13- by 9-inch baking pan.

Cook the lasagne noodles following the basic method (p. 13) until al dente. Rinse and drain well.

In a small bowl, combine the cilantro and flat-leaf parsley.

Assemble the lasagne: Cover the bottom of the prepared pan with 4 lasagne noodles. Spread half the calabacitas over the noodles. Top with the cooked chicken. Spread with a generous third of the

béchamel and sprinkle with a third of the shredded mozzarella and a third of the cilantro mixture. Cover with 4 more lasagne noodles, the remaining calabacitas, and half of the remaining béchamel. Sprinkle with half the remaining mozzarella and half the remaining cilantro mixture. Top with the remaining 4 noodles and cover with the remaining béchamel, mozzarella, and cilantro mixture. Cover the lasagne with foil.

Bake for 20 minutes. Remove the foil and bake for 20 to 25 minutes longer, or until the lasagne is bubbly and the edges are golden brown. Let stand for 10 minutes before slicing and serving.

12 uncooked fresh or dried lasagne noodles (12 ounces)

½ cup minced fresh cilantro

½ cup chopped fresh flat-leaf parsley

1½ pounds boneless, skinless chicken breasts, cooked & cut into 1- to 1½-inch strips

3 cups shredded mozzarella or Monterey Jack cheese

BAKED MACARONI WITH YELLOW SQUASH & FOUR CHEESES

SERVES 6

BÉCHAMEL SAUCE—WHAT OUR MOTHERS USED TO
CALL WHITE SAUCE—REMAINS THE PERFECT CHOICE FOR PROVIDING
CREAMINESS AND MELDING TOGETHER THE FLAVORS OF
THE FOUR CHEESES IN THIS MACARONI DISH. SUN-DRIED TOMATOES
AND RIBBONS OF YELLOW SQUASH ADD A LITTLE COLOR.

Preheat the oven to 350°F. Butter a 2-quart casserole dish.

Cook the macaroni following the basic method (p. 13) until al dente. Drain well.

Meanwhile, prepare the béchamel sauce: In a medium-size saucepan, melt the butter over medium heat. Add the garlic and cook for 30 seconds. Stir in the flour and cook, stirring, for about 1 minute, or until the mixture is bubbling and smooth. Gradually stir in the milk until well blended and smooth and cook, stirring constantly, for 1 to 2 minutes, or until the sauce has thickened slightly. Reduce the heat to low, season with the nutmeg and salt and pepper and cook for 3 to 4 minutes, until the sauce has thickened. Remove the saucepan from the heat.

In a large bowl, combine the macaroni, onion, sun-dried tomatoes, squash, and herbs and toss together until well mixed. Gently stir in the béchamel until the macaroni is well coated. Fold in all the cheeses. Spoon the mixture into the prepared casserole dish. Bake for about 30 to 35 minutes, or until lightly browned on top and bubbly. Let stand for 5 minutes before serving.

12 ounces dried large elbow
   macaroni

BÉCHAMEL SAUCE
4 tablespoons (½ stick) butter
1 garlic clove, minced
3 tablespoons all-purpose flour
2 cups milk
Pinch of grated nutmeg
Salt & freshly ground black
   pepper to taste

½ onion, chopped
½ cup sun-dried tomatoes, packed
   in oil, sliced
2 yellow squash, sliced lengthwise
   into ¼-inch-thick ribbons
¼ cup chopped fresh
   flat-leaf parsley
2 tablespoons minced fresh cilantro
2 tablespoons minced fresh basil
1 cup each shredded medium-sharp
   cheddar, fontina &
   Monterey Jack cheeses
1 cup freshly grated
   Parmesan cheese

SPICY SESAME NOODLE SALAD

SERVES 6

THE DISTINCTIVE EARTHINESS OF SOBA, OR
BUCKWHEAT, NOODLES IS WELL SUITED TO THE STRONG
FLAVORS OF TOASTED SESAME OIL, SOY SAUCE,
AND GARLIC. SMALL PORTIONS OF THIS SIDE SALAD
ARE PERFECTLY SATISFYING.

Cook the noodles following the basic method (p. 13) until just barely al dente. Drain well.

Prepare the dressing: In a small skillet, toast the sesame seeds and hot pepper flakes over medium-high heat, stirring frequently, for 1 to 2 minutes, or until the seeds are golden brown and aromatic. Transfer to a plate to cool.

In a food processor fitted with the metal blade, combine the soy sauce, honey, peanut butter, sesame oil, vinegar, and garlic and process until smooth. Add the toasted sesame seed and hot pepper flake mixture and pulse briefly just to mix.

Prepare the salad: In a medium-size bowl, combine the noodles, dressing, green onion, and chopped cilantro and gently toss together. Divide the noodles among serving plates and garnish with the cucumber and avocado slices. Sprinkle with the cilantro leaves and toasted sesame seeds.

1 (7-ounce) package Japanese soba (buckwheat) noodles or 7 ounces dried whole-wheat spaghetti, linguine, or vermicelli

SESAME DRESSING

3 tablespoons white sesame seeds

½ teaspoon hot pepper flakes

⅓ cup soy sauce

1½ teaspoons honey

1 tablespoon natural peanut butter

2 tablespoons Asian sesame oil

1 tablespoon balsamic vinegar

2 garlic cloves, minced

SALAD

1 green onion, chopped

¼ cup coarsely chopped fresh cilantro

½ cucumber, seeded & cut crosswise into ¼-inch-thick slices

1 large ripe avocado, peeled, seeded & sliced lengthwise

Fresh cilantro, for garnish

Toasted white sesame seeds, for garnish

ORZO & CORN SALAD WITH
RED CHILE VINAIGRETTE

HERE RED CHILE MEANS PURE GROUND NEW MEXICAN
RED CHILES, NOT BOTTLED CHILE POWDER, OR CHILE BLENDS. IF RED
CHILE IS NOT AVAILABLE, LOOK FOR GROUND ANCHO OR POBLANO
CHILES, OR CHILE PASILLA. IF YOU MUST SUBSTITUTE CHILE POWDER OR
A CHILE BLEND, REDUCE THE AMOUNT TO A SCANT 1 TEASPOON.

RED CHILE VINAIGRETTE

1 tablespoon plus 2 teaspoons
  pure ground red chiles,
  mild or medium-hot

½ teaspoon cumin seeds

2 garlic cloves, minced

Juice of 2 limes

¼ cup red wine vinegar

¼ cup minced fresh cilantro

¼ cup chopped fresh
  flat-leaf parsley

⅔ cup olive oil

ORZO SALAD

12 ounces dried orzo

1½ cups cooked pink beans,
  pinto beans, or cranberry
  beans, or 1 (15-ounce) can
  beans, drained & rinsed

1½ cups corn kernels, cooked fresh
  or thawed frozen

3 green onions, chopped

3 ripe plum tomatoes, diced

Salt & freshly ground black
  pepper to taste

Prepare the vinaigrette: In a small bowl, whisk together the ground chiles, cumin seeds, garlic, lime juice, vinegar, cilantro, and parsley. Add the oil in a steady stream, whisking constantly until emulsified. Set aside.

Prepare the salad: Cook the orzo following the basic method (p. 13) until al dente. Drain well, rinse with cold water and drain again.

In a large bowl, combine the orzo, beans, corn, green onions, and tomatoes. Add the vinaigrette and toss to mix well. Season with the salt and pepper. Serve at room temperature or chilled. Tightly covered, the orzo salad can be refrigerated one day.

SHRIMP & PASTA SALAD WITH RED PEPPER VINAIGRETTE

SERVES 6

TO SERVE, SPOON EACH SALAD ONTO A BED OF MIXED
GREENS OR INTO A RADICCHIO LEAF "CUP." COMPLETE THE PLATE
WITH GRILLED TOMATO SLICES AND CRUSTY ITALIAN BREAD
FOR A SIMPLE BUT PERFECT LUNCH. THE SALAD CAN BE MADE AHEAD;
TOSS IT AGAIN JUST BEFORE SERVING.

Prepare the mayonnaise: in a food processor fitted with the metal blade, purée the roasted bell pepper. Transfer the pepper to a small bowl. Add the remaining ingredients and stir to mix well. Cover and refrigerate.

Cook the pasta following the basic method (p. 13) until al dente. Drain well, rinse with cold water and drain again.

In a large bowl, combine the pasta, shrimp, peas, zucchini, green onions, parsley, tarragon, and hot pepper flakes and toss until well mixed. Stir in the mayonnaise and season with the salt and pepper. Serve chilled.

RED BELL PEPPER MAYONNAISE

½ Roasted Red Bell Pepper (p. 20), cored, seeded, peeled & chopped

1 cup mayonnaise

2 tablespoons tarragon vinegar

1 garlic clove, minced

2 teaspoons Dijon mustard

1 tablespoon tomato paste

Salt & freshly ground black pepper to taste

1 pound dried medium-size conchiglie

1 pound large shrimp, cooked & shelled

1½ cups peas, cooked fresh or thawed frozen

1 zucchini, halved lengthwise & thinly sliced crosswise

2 green onions, chopped

2 tablespoons chopped fresh flat-leaf parsley

1 tablespoon plus 1 teaspoon minced fresh tarragon leaves

1 teaspoon hot pepper flakes

Salt & freshly ground black pepper to taste

TORTELLINI SALAD WITH
GRILLED TOMATO VINAIGRETTE

SERVES 6

As with many simple dishes, this vibrant
tortellini salad is entirely dependent on the quality
of the ingredients. In this case try to shop in
an Italian market or specialty food shop so you can
get the best quality salami and provolone.

TOMATO VINAIGRETTE

2 ripe plum tomatoes

1 tablespoon tomato paste

1 garlic clove, minced

3 tablespoons red wine vinegar

3 tablespoons balsamic vinegar

2 teaspoons Dijon mustard

1 teaspoon honey

⅓ cup extra-virgin olive oil

⅓ cup vegetable oil

Salt & pepper to taste

1 pound cheese, mushroom,
    spinach, or other tortellini

¾ cup julienned provolone cheese

2 ounces sliced Italian hard salami

⅔ cup thinly sliced celery

¼ cup Calamata olives,
    halved & pitted

½ cup julienned red or
    green bell pepper

1 tablespoon chopped red onion

2 teaspoons capers

¼ cup chopped fresh
    flat-leaf parsley

1 teaspoon minced fresh rosemary

1 tablespoon fresh lemon juice

Salt & pepper to taste

Prepare the vinaigrette: Prepare a grill or preheat the broiler, with the pan 6 inches from the heat source. Halve the tomatoes lengthwise. Grill the tomatoes, skin side down, or broil, skin side up, for 2 to 4 minutes, or until the skin is wrinkled and partially blackened.

Transfer the tomatoes to a food processor fitted with the metal blade. Add the tomato paste, garlic, vinegars, mustard, and honey and process for 15 to 30 seconds, or until smooth. With the machine running, add the olive oil and then the vegetable oil in a thin, steady stream. Season with the salt and pepper.

Cook the tortellini until al dente. Cooking time will vary; watch the tortellini closely and test often for doneness. Drain, rinse under cold running water to stop the cooking, and drain well. Let cool.

In a large bowl, combine the tortellini, provolone, salami, celery, olives, bell pepper, onion, capers, parsley, rosemary, and lemon juice and gently toss together. Drizzle the vinaigrette over the salad and toss to coat. Season with the salt and pepper. Serve immediately or refrigerate, covered. Let come to room temperature before serving. The salad will keep for up to one day.

POPPY SEED KUGEL

SERVES 4 TO 6

KUGEL (THE NAME MEANS PUDDING IN YIDDISH) IS A
TRADITIONAL EASTERN EUROPEAN DESSERT. IT IS BEST EATEN WARM;
ONCE BAKED, COVER AND KEEP IT IN A WARM OVEN
UNTIL READY TO SERVE. FOR A MORE TANGY RESULT, SUBSTITUTE SOUR
CREAM OR YOGURT FOR THE RICOTTA OR COTTAGE CHEESE.

6 ounces dried wide egg noodles

2 cups milk

2 large eggs

½ cup sugar

2 tablespoons cornstarch

2 tablespoons butter, at
  room temperature

1 teaspoon grated lemon zest

1 tablespoon poppy seeds

⅔ cup ricotta cheese or cottage
  cheese, puréed in a food
  processor

⅓ cup seedless golden raisins or
  dried cherries (optional)

Unsweetened whipped cream
  (optional)

Cook the noodles following the basic method (p. 13) until al dente. Drain well.

Preheat the oven to 350°F. Lightly grease a 2-quart casserole or 9-inch-square baking dish.

In a medium-size saucepan, heat the milk over medium heat just until bubbles appear around the edge of the saucepan. Remove from the heat.

In a small bowl, whisk together the eggs, sugar, and cornstarch. Add half the hot milk, whisking constantly. Pour the egg mixture into the hot milk remaining in the saucepan, return the pan to medium heat, and bring to a boil, stirring constantly with a wooden spoon. Then boil, until thickened, about 1 minute. Remove from the heat and stir in the butter, lemon zest, and poppy seeds.

In a large bowl, stir together the noodles, custard mixture, ricotta or cream cheese, and the golden raisins or dried cherries, if desired, until well combined. Transfer the mixture into the prepared baking dish. Bake for 25 to 30 minutes, or until bubbly and the edges are lightly browned. Serve warm, with unsweetened whipped cream if desired.

SWEET FARFALLE FRITTERS

MAKES 40 COOKIES

THE ADDITION OF CONFECTIONERS' SUGAR AND OIL MAKES
THIS PASTA SLIGHTLY SILKY AND SWEET, PERFECT FOR THESE CRUNCHY COOKIE-
LIKE FRITTERS. KEEP THE FRYING OIL AT THE PROPER TEMPERATURE
TO PRODUCE LIGHT, FLAKY COOKIES. THEY ARE BEST EATEN FRESH, BUT CAN
BE STORED IN AN AIRTIGHT CONTAINER FOR A DAY.

In the bowl of an electric pasta machine, combine the flour, sugar, anise, and salt, and mix for about 30 seconds. With the machine running, slowly add the oil, then the eggs, egg yolk, and vanilla extract. Knead for about 2 minutes, then check the dough: It should feel slightly more elastic than pasta dough (p. 12); if necessary, add more flour or water, teaspoon by teaspoon. Continue to knead for a total of 8 to 10 minutes.

Extrude the dough with the disk for lasagne noodles and cut into 3-inch lengths. Pinch the centers together into bow-tie shapes and place on a floured baking sheet. Or prepare the dough by hand and cut into lasagne noodles (p. 14). Cut into 3-inch lengths and pinch as above.

In a large heavy skillet, deep-fat fryer, or electric skillet, heat 2 to 3 inches of oil to 375°F. (The oil will sizzle when a scrap of dough is added, and the dough will puff and bubble almost immediately; the oil should not be smoking hot). Fry 5 or 6 fritters at a time, for about 30 seconds on each side, or until crisp and golden brown. With a slotted spoon, remove the fritters to a wire rack placed over paper towels to drain.

Place about 2 cups confectioners' sugar in a paper bag. Add the farfalle, a few at a time, shaking gently to coat them. Garnish with fresh raspberries.

1⅔ cups all-purpose flour

½ cup confectioners' sugar

½ teaspoon ground anise

⅛ teaspoon salt

1 tablespoon vegetable oil

2 large eggs

1 large egg yolk

1 teaspoon pure vanilla extract

Vegetable oil, for deep-frying

Confectioners' sugar & fresh raspberries, for garnish

APRICOT-FILLED RAVIOLI WITH SWEET SPICED CRÈME ANGLAISE

THESE RAVIOLI CAN EVEN BE SERVED ON
THEIR OWN AS TINY FILLED PASTRIES OR COOKIES, WITHOUT
THE SAUCE. IF THE CRÈME ANGLAISE SEEMS
TOO THICK AFTER CHILLING, SIMPLY POUR IT INTO A FOOD
PROCESSOR AND PROCESS UNTIL SMOOTH.

SPICED CRÈME ANGLAISE

1¾ cups half-and-half

3 tablespoons granulated sugar

4 large egg yolks

½ teaspoon ground cinnamon

¼ teaspoon grated nutmeg

⅛ teaspoon ground allspice

2 tablespoons rum

APRICOT FILLING

8 ounces dried apricots

2 tablespoons rum

2 tablespoons honey

2 tablespoons granulated sugar

2 tablespoons grated orange zest

Prepare the crème anglaise: In a saucepan, heat the half-and-half with 1 tablespoon of the granulated sugar until bubbles appear. Remove the pan from the heat.

In a bowl, whisk together the egg yolks and the remaining 2 tablespoons granulated sugar and add the spices, whisking constantly. Add the hot cream, then pour the egg mixture back into the saucepan. Return the saucepan to medium heat and cook, stirring constantly, for 2 to 3 minutes, or until the custard coats the back of a spoon. Strain through a sieve. Stir in the rum, cover, and refrigerate.

Prepare the filling: In a non-reactive saucepan, combine all the ingredients and ½ cup water. Bring to a boil, stirring often. Reduce the heat to low and simmer for 6 minutes, or until the apricots are soft and most of the liquid is absorbed. Remove from the heat and let cool slightly. Transfer the mixture to a food processor fitted with the metal blade and pulse for 5 seconds, until the apricots are finely chopped.

Prepare the dough: In the food processor, combine the flour, sugar, and salt and pulse to combine. Add the cream cheese and butter and process until crumbly. Add the egg yolk and extract and process until the dough forms a ball. Transfer to a lightly floured work surface and knead several times. Cover the dough with plastic wrap and

refrigerate for 30 minutes. Preheat the oven to 375°F. Lightly grease a baking sheet.

On a lightly floured work surface, roll the dough into a rectangle about 20 inches wide by 18 inches long, following the basic method (p. 14). Cut the dough into rounds with a 3½-inch round cutter.

Spoon a generous teaspoon of the filling into the center of each round. Lightly moisten the edges of each round with water, and fold over into a half-moon shape. Using a fork, seal the edges. Place the ravioli on the prepared baking sheet. Bake for 12 to 14 minutes, or until the bottoms are golden brown and the tops are lightly colored. Cool.

Dust each plate with 1 to 2 tablespoons of confectioners' sugar. Place 4 ravioli on each plate to create a square in the center of the plate. Spoon 2 or 3 tablespoons of crème anglaise in the center of the plate. Garnish with raspberries and apricots, if desired. Serve immediately.

SWEET RAVIOLI DOUGH

1¼ cups all-purpose flour

¼ cup granulated sugar

¼ teaspoon salt

4 ounces cream cheese, chilled
    & cut into small pieces

4 tablespoons (½ stick) unsalted
    butter, chilled & cut into
    small pieces

1 large egg yolk

½ teaspoon pure vanilla extract

Confectioners' sugar

Fresh raspberries & chopped dried
    apricots, for garnish (optional)

INDEX

CONVERSION TABLE

WEIGHTS

ounces & pounds	metric equivalents
¼ ounce	7 grams
⅓ ounce	10 g
½ ounce	14 g
1 ounce	28 g
1½ ounces	42 g
1¾ ounces	50 g
2 ounces	57 g
3 ounces	85 g
3½ ounces	100 g
4 ounces (¼ pound)	114 g
6 ounces	170 g
8 ounces (½ pound)	227 g
9 ounces	250 g
16 ounces (1 pound)	464 g

TEMPERATURES

°F (Fahrenheit)	°C (Celsius or Centigrade)
32 (water freezes)	0
200	93.3
212 (water boils)	100
250	120
275	135
300 (slow oven)	150
325	160
350 (moderate oven)	175
375	190
400 (hot oven)	205
425	220
450 (very hot oven)	233
475	245
500 (extremely hot oven)	260

LIQUID MEASURES

spoons & cups	metric equivalents
¼ teaspoon	1.23 mm
½ teaspoon	2.5 mm
¾ teaspoon	3.7 mm
1 teaspoon	5 mm
1 dessertspoon	10 mm
1 tablespoon (3 teaspoons)	15 mm
2 tablespoons (1 ounce)	30 mm
¼ cup	60 mm
⅓ cup	80 mm
½ cup	120 mm
⅔ cup	160 mm
¾ cup	180 mm
1 cup (8 ounces)	240 mm
2 cups (1 pint)	480 mm
3 cups	710 mm
4 cups (1 quart)	1 liter
4 quarts (1 gallon)	3¾ liters

LENGTH

U.S. measurements	metric equivalents
⅛ inch	3 mm
¼ inch	6 mm
⅜ inch	1 cm
½ inch	1.2 cm
¾ inch	2 cm
1 inch	2.5 cm
1¼ inches	3.1 cm
1½ inches	3.7 cm
2 inches	5 cm
3 inches	7.5 cm
4 inches	10 cm
5 inches	12.5 cm

APPROXIMATE EQUIVALENTS

1 kilo is slightly more than 2 pounds
1 liter is slightly more than 1 quart
1 meter is slightly over 3 feet
1 centimeter is approximately ⅜ inch